Appletree Guides

IRISH FIRST NAMES

RONAN COGHLAN

Contents

Acknowledgements

I would like to extend my thanks to a number of people who have helped me with the preparation of this work: to my sisters, Lin and Valerie, who provided help in compiling the statistics and in preparing the typescript; to Leslie Dunkling for pointing out a number of errors in the work; and to Eileen Ryan of St Andrews, Scotland, who provided me with details of some unusual Irish feminine names. The principal institutions in which research for this work was carried out were the Library of Trinity College, Dublin, and the National Library of Ireland, Dublin.

Published and printed by
The Appletree Press Ltd
7 James Street South
Belfast BT2 8DL
1985

9 8 7 6 5 4 3 2

British Library Cataloguing in Publication Data
Coghlan, Ronan
Irish first names.
1. Names, Personal—Irish—Dictionaries
I. Title
929.4'4'09415   050CS2375.17

ISBN 0-86281-153-8

Introduction

Since the publication in 1923 of Father Patrick Woulfe's *Irish Names for Children*, no work on Irish first names has appeared in print. When Woulfe wrote the Irish, especially in the country districts, were exceedingly conservative in their choice of names. Woulfe hoped to broaden the selection of names in use. To do this he included a number of older Irish names, as well as names generally in use at the time.

His work was undoubtedly influential. Ireland had attained independence in 1921 and a spirit of nationalism was rampant. People began seeking out old Gaelic names to give their children, and they found Woulfe's work a handy quarry. Since his time Irish naming patterns have changed so considerably that a new work on the subject is again needed.

The greatest changes have taken place in recent years. Even after Woulfe's work had appeared, names such as *John, William, Mary* and *Annie* were still the commonest names in Irish households. However, these names are now rapidly falling from favour, giving way to a host of newcomers, many of them exotic.

I have had to use certain criteria for selecting names to include in this book. I have included all names which originated in the Irish language and whose derivations I was able to trace. Various early names which are no longer in use, but which are of historical interest, are listed at the end of the book. I have also included a number of names which sprang from the fertile imaginations of Irish writers. Names in this category include *Vanessa* and *Gloria*, which are widespread today.

The original language of the Celts, in prehistoric times, split into two branches, the Goidelic and the Brythonic. Irish, Scottish Gaelic and Manx belong to the former; Welsh, Cornish and Breton to the latter. The Irish language is sometimes called Gaelic, but this can lead to confusion with the Scottish Gaelic. (The word Gaelic, incidentally, is pronounced *Gaylik* in Ireland, *Gallik* in Scotland and the languages are mutually intelligible.) Irish is also sometimes wrongly called Erse – a word looked on with distaste by the Irish themselves.

Irish was the principal language of the country until the mid-nineteenth century. When people wanted to 'translate' their names into English, they frequently used an English name that bore some resemblance – often phonetic – to their own, for example, *Jeremiah* and *Cornelius* were used as equivalents of *Dermot* and *Connor*. In this way non-Irish names like *Daniel, Denis* and *Hugh* came to be established in Ireland.

Reference is made in the text to 'Hiberno-English': this is a term employed by linguists to describe the species of English spoken in Ireland today. It is supplanting the older 'Anglo-Irish'.

Where appropriate, I have given the Irish translation of the English name, usually after it. The Irish form often differs from the English, and sometimes it is the version given at the registration of the child's birth.

There are a few basic rules to bear in mind when pronouncing Irish names. Letters in Irish have the same phonetic values as in English with the following exceptions:

a is pronounced like *o* in cot
á is pronounced like *aw* in paw
bh is pronounced like *v* (or *w*)
c is always hard, as in cattle
ch is pronounced like *ch* as in Bach
dh is pronounced like *y*
e is unpronounced before *a,* unless accented
é is pronounced like *ay* in play
fh is unpronounced
g is hard as in tiger
gh is pronounced like *y*
i is pronounced like *ee* in seek
mh is prounoued like *v* or *w*
ó is prounounded like *o* in go
s is pronounced *sh* before *e* or *i*
sh is pronounced like *h*
th is pronounced like *h*
ú is pronounced like *oo* in zoo

In each article I have given the derivation and history of the name, with particular reference to its usage in Ireland. Derivations cannot always be regarded as certain, especially as some names are so old that their roots are almost impossible to uncover. Take, for example, the name *Adam*. The standard authority on English Christian names, Withycombe, says this is a Hebrew name, meaning 'red'; yet there is evidence that the name means 'man'; and it may not even be Hebrew at all, but Akkadian, meaning 'creature'.

Parents may be interested in some ideas about choosing a name. One of the first considerations is how a first name will sound when coupled with a surname. A very 'Irish' surname is ill-mated with an exotic forename. Such combinations as *Desirée Mulligan, Heinrich Rafferty,* and *Ludovico MacGonigle* are to be discouraged. Secondly, the number of syllables in a surname will determine how well a first name will go with it. If your surname has two syllables, a three-syllable first name will probably suit it best.

Parents in Ireland are free of legal restrictions when it comes to naming their offspring. By contrast, in France there is a prescribed list from which a Christian name has to be chosen; in West Germany, if you want to bestow a first name of which the Registrar has not heard, you have to show that the name has been used before; while in Brazil, you will not be allowed to confer a name likely to bring ridicule on the bearer. This last is a sensible rule. Much – I suspect rather too much – has been made of the psychological effects a child's name may have on it. However, it is a good idea to remember a few points:

(a) Don't give your child the same name as one of his parents. Learning his name and how it is distinct from others' will help him to develop his sense of individuality. If he shares his name with someone else in the family, the growth of his individuality may suffer. For the same reason, it is unwise to give children in the same family similar names (e.g. *Jane* and *Joan*).

(b) Don't give your child a name which, coupled with its surname, may produce mirth, e.g. *Iva Bunyan, Robin Banks*.

(c) If your surname is that of someone famous in history or literature, don't give your child that person's first name. Mr and Mrs *Ripper* should not call their child *Jack;* and Mr and Mrs *Joyce* should eschew *James*.

(d) Don't give your child a name which makes its sex doubtful. It is particularly inadvisable to name boys *Evelyn* or *Hilary*. *Florence* is still found as a boys' name in parts of Ireland. If a child with this name is ever taken overseas, think of the jibes he will receive from his peers.

(e) One wonders if it is wise to choose a first name which rhymes with a child's surname, e.g. *Jill Hill*. In fact, there is in the United States a body called the 'My Name is a Poem' Club, all members having names that rhyme with their surnames. Ed McBain, the detective story writer, created a sleuth whose father, as a practical joke, gave him the same name as his surname for his first name. He went through life known as *Meyer Meyer* and went prematurely bald.

Does a book like this help anyone other than parents? I believe it does. Naming patterns change and continue, forming a history. I hope, for instance, that this book will assist the writer looking for unusual or historical names. I remember once being irritated to find, in Cecilia Holland's novel *The Kings in Winter,* set in the time of Brian Boru, characters named *Sean* and *Liam.* Irish names, yes – but you would not have found them in Ireland in the eleventh century.

In early times the names used in Ireland reflected the heroic spirit of the age – names such as *Murrough,* 'sea warrior', *Cathal*, 'battle mighty' and *Niall*, 'champion'. Many of these names have been revived in the twentieth century. Later, the Christians would choose the name of a saint for their offspring and prefix to it *mael* or *gille*, meaning 'servant' – a pattern which is still continued today amongst Roman Catholics in Ireland, although nowadays the prefix is seldom found. The Vikings brought with them Norse names such as *Olaf*, which spread widely in its Gaelic form *Amhlaoibh*. The Normans, who invaded Ireland in 1169, introduced a host of new names, e.g. *Edward, Gerald, William, Pierce*.

It is my hope that this book will fill a gap and provide a comprehensive dictionary of the names found in Ireland; and even that it may help to revive some of the rarer names that it contains.

Irish First Names

Aaron [*Árón*] (m) This name comes from the Bible. It was borne by the brother of Moses in the Old Testament, and it is possibly of Egyptian origin. The meaning 'high mountain' has been suggested. It is sometimes used in Ireland today.

Abigail [*Abaigeal*] (f) 'father rejoiced'. A name which, in Ireland, was used to anglicise the native name, *Gobinet*.

Abraham [*Ábraham*] (m) Hebrew, 'father of a multitude'. The name has occasionally been used in Ireland, e.g. by Abraham ('Bram') Stoker, author of *Dracula* (1897). *Abracham* is another Gaelic form.

Abram (m) Hebrew, 'high father'. This was the name originally borne by Abraham in the Old Testament. It was used in the *Clibborn* family of Moate Castle, Co. Westmeath.

Achaius (m) A form of *Eochaidh*, mainly used in Scotland.

Adam [*Ádhamh*] (m) A name of uncertain meaning. 'Red earth' and 'ruddy' have been suggested, but it possibly signifies 'man'. Adam has been quite a popular name in Ireland, where is appears to have been in use from early times. The Hebrews themselves do not seem to have bestowed the name, and its use as a Christian name probably started with the early Irish and Scottish Christians.

Adamnan [*Adhamhnan*] (m) 'little Adam'. The name of an important Irish saint (*c.* 624-704), the biographer of St Columba and an acquaintance of the Venerable Bede. He is the first known writer to speak of a monster in Loch Ness. There are many variants of the name, e.g. *Awnan, Odanodan, O(u)nan, Junan* which are given under separate headings.

Adrian [*Aidrian*] (m) Latin, 'of the Adriatic'. In its original form, *Hadrianus*, this was the name of a well-known Roman emperor. The name seems quite popular in Ireland today.

Aeneas [*Aenéas*] (m) Greek, 'worthy of praise'. The name of a character in Homer's *Iliad* who became the hero of Virgil's *Aeneid*. It has been used in Ireland to anglicise the native name *Aengus*, 'one vigour'.

Aengus [*Aonghus*] (m) 'one vigour'. This early name, still found in Ireland, was once often used. Aengus of the Birds was the love god of the pagan Irish. St Aengus the Culdee was a well-known bearer of the name. Another form probably occurs in Arthurian romance, borne by King *Anguish* of Ireland. *Aeneas* was used as a substitute name. The Scottish form of Aengus, *Angus*, is also found in Ireland. The variants *Oengus, Hungus, Ungus* and *Enos* are also found.

Afric (f) Variant of *Africa*.

Africa [*Aifric*] (f) 'pleasant'. This name has no connection with the continent of Africa. Its associations are with both Ireland and the Isle of Man, where its use is recorded in the eleventh and twelfth centuries. The daughter of the Manx monarch, Godred, bore the name. Another king of Man, Olaus the Swarthy, married Africa, daughter of Fergus of Galway. *Afric* is a variant.

Agatha [*Agata*] (f) Greek, 'good'. The name of a third-century Sicilian martyr.

Aghy (m) A form of *Eochaidh*.

Agnes [*Aignéis*] (f) Greek, 'pure'. This name was brought to Ireland by the English. It is sometimes equated with *Una*, perhaps because it was thought to derive from the Latin *agnus*, 'lamb', the Irish for lamb being *uan*. The name *Ina* (Irish *Aghna*) may be a native form of Agnes.

Aichlinn (m) There was a harper named Aichlinn competing in the Harpers' Meeting which was held in Belfast in 1792. It is perhaps a form of *Echlin*.

Aidan [*Aodhan*] (m) 'little fire'. St Aidan (died 651), a monk at Iona who became bishop of Lindisfarne, is perhaps the most famous bearer of this name. It was quite common in Ireland in the eighth and ninth centuries and it is still used today. *Mogue* is a variant. It has even been employed as a feminine name, but *Edana* is the more usual feminine form. A modern bearer is the Irish actor, Aidan Grinnell.

Aideen (f) Variant of *Etain*.

Aileen (f) Variant of *Eileen*.

Ailill (m) 'sprite'. It was a common name in early times. Ailill Molt was an early Irish king.

Áine (f) 'joy'; 'praise'; also 'fasting'. Áine was said to be the queen of the South Munster fairies, living at Knockany (Irish *Cnoc Áine* – Áine's hill'). The name is still used in Ireland. It has tended to become confused with *Anne*. There have been various attempts to anglicise it as *Anna, Hannah* and, perhaps, *Anastasia*.

Ainmire (m) 'great lord'. A name which occurs quite frequently in Irish history. It was borne by St Ainmire, a monk of Co. Donegal, and by Ainmire, king of Tara (died c. 569).

Alan [*Ailín*] (m) Woulfe regards this as an early Irish name, perhaps connected with *ail*, 'noble', but the name is by no means confined to Ireland. It may have been the name of a Celtic deity, the brother of Bran; compare also the Welsh *Alawn*, 'harmony'. Its use in England and Scotland can be traced to Alan Fergeant, Count of Brittany, who came to England with the Conqueror. In English lore, Alan-a-Dale is associated with Robin Hood. Alan is frequently encountered in Ireland today. *Allan* and *Allen* are variants. Allen was used by the novelist Rider Haggard for his hero, Allen Quartermain.

Alana (f) Also spelt *Alannah*. This is not the feminine of

Alan – though in Scotland it is often treated as such – but it comes from the Irish *a leanbh*, 'O child'. It is not a common name.

Alastrina [*Alastríona*] (f) A feminine of *Alistair*. In Irish *Alastríona* translates *Alexandra* and *Alexandrina*.

Albany (m) The Irish name *Fionn* (English *Finn)* came from *find*, 'white' or 'fair'. This was anglicised as *Albany*, from Latin *albus*, 'white'.

Albert (m) Germanic, 'noble bright'. In Ireland this name has been used as an anglicisation of *Ailbe* (English *Alby)*. It appears to be little used today.

Alby [*Ailbe*] (m) The name of an Irish saint. It has sometimes been anglicised as *Albert*. *Ailbhe* is a variant in Irish; *Elli* and *Elly* are variants in English.

Alexander [*Alastar*] (m) Greek, 'helper of man'. A popular name in the Hellenic world: it was the name of Alexander the Great, king of Macedonia, and it was also another name given to the Trojan prince, Paris. A number of early saints were called Alexander. The name spread widely, becoming *Alexandre* in French, *Alessandro* in Italian and *Alejandro* in Spanish. It seems to have been brought to Scotland by Queen Margaret (*c.* 1046-93), who was raised in Hungary, and who gave the name to one of her sons. The English brought it to Ireland, where it throve amongst the settlers of the Middle Ages. *Alastar* became the normal Gaelic form; *Alsander, Alastrann* and *Alastrom* were also used.

Alfred [*Ailfrid*] (m) Anglo-Saxon, 'elf counsel'. This name was imported into Ireland by the English. It is established, but not common.

Alice [*Ailís*] (f) Old French *Aliz*, coming ultimately from Germanic *Adelaide*, 'noble sort'. The name was introduced into Ireland by the English. A medieval Irish example is Alice Kettler, who figured in a witchcraft trial. It is perhaps, but by no means certainly, the origin of an Irish name *Aylce*. Lewis Carroll's *Alice's Adventures in Wonderland* (1865) greatly increased the popularity of the name. See also *Alicia, Alison*.

Alicia [*Ailíse*] (f) A latinised form of Alice, occasionally used in Ireland.

Alison [*Allsún*] (f) A diminutive of *Alice*, in use at least from the thirteenth century, when it was recorded in France. It has occasionally been employed in Ireland.

Alistair (m) An anglicised form of *Alastar*, the Gaelic for *Alexander*.

Alma (f) 'all good'. An early Irish name; but its modern usage can be traced to diverse origins – it is the feminine of Latin *almus*, 'loving' or 'good' and, as such, it is applied to the Blessed Virgin. St Alma, the mother of St Tudwal, may derive her name from this source. Alma, as used by Spenser in *The Faerie Queene* (1590/6), comes from the Italian meaning 'soul', though Spenser may have heard the Irish name during his stay in Ireland. In later times, Alma was used in England after the Battle of Alma (1854) in the Crimean War. The name of the River Alma, where the battle was fought, may have been Celtic in origin.

Alma became popular in the United States in the 1920 s and was exported from there to Britain. In this instance it probably came from the Latin, as in *alma mater,* a title originally applied to classical goddesses and later to academic institutions.

Alma occurs as a masculine name in Irish legend: Alma One-Tooth was the name of a son of Nemed. Alma is also a masculine name in the Book of Mormon.

Aloysius [*Alaois*] (m) Like *Ludovicus,* a Latin form of *Louis,* borne of St Aloysius Gonzaga (died 1591; canonised 1726). In everyday life he was known by the Italian form *Luigi.* Aloysius was introduced into Ireland in commemoration of him, and it was used to translate *Lughaidh.* Its Gaelic forms are *Alaois, Alabhaois.*

Alphonsus [*Alfonsus*] (m) Germanic, 'noble ready'. This name was introduced into Ireland to commemorate St Alphonsus Liguori (1696-1787; canonised 1839). It has sometimes been used to anglicise *Anlon.*

Alvy (f) Variant of *Elva.*

Amalgith [*Amalgaid*] (m) According to the Welsh chronicler, Nennius, Amalgith was a man whose seven sons were baptised by St Patrick. It is said that their descendants, the Ui Amalgaid, gave their name to Tirawley *(Tir Amalgaid).* The surname *Macaulay* is connected with them. As a result of Norse influence, *Amhlaoibh* came to replace this name.

Amanda (f) This name, apparently a literary invention, is now quite widespread in Ireland. It comes from Latin and means 'worthy of love'. It is first recorded in Cibber's play *Love's Last Shift* (1694). *Mandy* is a pet form.

Ambrose [*Ambrós*] (m) Greek, 'immortal'. The name of a saintly bishop of Milan (*c.* 340-97). In Ireland it was used to anglicise the native name, *Anmchadh.*

Anastasia [*Anstás*] (f) Greek, 'risen once more'. This name occurs in England in the thirteenth century. It spread from there to Ireland. It is still used from time to time in Ireland but it appears to be sharply declining in popularity. The pet form is *Stasia* (Irish, *Steise).*

André (m) The French form of *Andrew* which has sometimes been used in Ireland in modern times.

Andrea (f) A feminine form of *Andrew,* increasingly popular in Ireland in modern times.

Andrew [*Aindréas*] (m) Greek, 'manly'. The name of one of the twelve Apostles. It was probably introduced into Ireland after the Norman Invasion of 1169. The Irish forms are *Aindreas* and *Aindrias* (forms which show an affinity with the original Greek *Andreas),* and *Aindriu,* which comes

from the Norman French *Andreu* (modern French *André*).
Andrew is a popular name in Ireland today. *Andy* and *Drew*
are pet forms of this name.

Aneas (m) This unusual name was borne by one Aneas
McDonnell (1783-1858), a native of Westport, Co. Mayo.
It is presumably a form of *Aeneas* or *Aengus*.

Angela [*Aingeal*] (f) Latin *Angela*, feminine of *angelus*,
'angel', from Greek *angelos*, 'messenger', corresponding to
Hebrew *malak*. Angela is quite a popular name in modern
Ireland. *Angie* is used as a pet form. The masculine form
is *Angelo*; compare the Arabic feminine name *Melek*,
'angel'.

Angus (m) This is the Scottish form of the Irish name
Aengus; but it is used in Ireland too. The Scots, who have
a habit of coining feminine equivalents to masculine names,
have produced the female *Angusina*.

Anita (f) The Spanish diminutive of *Anne* which is used in
Ireland.

Anlon [*Anluan*] (m) 'great champion'. Woulfe informs us
that this name was confined to a few families, notably the
O'Briens. See also *Alphonsus*.

Anmcha [*Anmchadh*] (m) 'courageous'. This name was
confined to the *O'Madden* family.

Anna (f) A form of *Anne* found in many European
languages, including Irish. It was employed in Ireland to
anglicise the native name *Áine*. The Irish actress, Anna
Manahan, is a contemporary example of this name.

Annabel [*Annábla*] (f) The Irish *Annábla* translates
Annabel, *Annabella* and *Arabella* – names of obscure origin
associated with Scotland, and introduced into Ireland in the
twelfth century after the Norman Invasion.

Annabella (f) See *Annabel*.

Anne [*Anna*] (f) Hebrew, 'He has favoured me'. St Anne
is the traditional name of the mother of the Blessed Virgin.
Anna, great-granddaughter of a Byzantine emperor,
brought the name to Western Europe by her marriage to
Henry I, king of France. Anne is very popular in Ireland
today. It has been used to some extent to anglicise the native
name *Áine*. *Nancy* is a pet form. See also *Anna* and *Annie*.

Annette (f) The French diminutive of *Anne* which seems to
be established in Ireland.

Annie (f) Originally this was a pet form of *Anne* but it is
now used as a separate name. In Ireland it was employed
to anglicise the native name *Ethna* (Irish *Eithne*).

Ant(h)ony [*Antaine*] (m) A Roman sept name of unknown
derivation. There are various Irish forms: *Antaine, Antoine,
Anntoin* and *Antoin*. Anthony was sometimes used to
anglicise *Uaithne* and *Hewney*. It has only become popular
in Ireland in modern times.

Aodh (m) 'fire'. Once a popular Irish name which was
anglicised as *Hugh*. It was latinised as *Aedus, Aidus* – the

name of a number of saints. It gave rise to the surname *MacAodha,* variously translated as *Magee* or *MacHugh* in Ireland, and *Mackay* in Scotland. Aodh (or Hugh) O'Neill and Oadh Rua (Red Hugh) O'Donnell were two famous Irish rebels who raised an insurrection in the reign of Elizabeth I. The name was also borne by six kings of Tara. The variant *Ea* occurs, and *Y* has been recorded.

Aodhfin [*Aodhfionn*] (m) 'white fire'. An early name.

Archibald (m) Germanic, 'simple bold'. A name which was used in Ulster and Scotland to anglicise *Giolla Easpaig. Archie* is a pet form.

Ardal [*Ardál*] (m) 'high valour'. An old historic name, which finally gave way to anglicisation as *Arnold.* See also *Artegal, Arthgallo.*

Arnold (m) Germanic, 'eagle power'. A name used in Ireland to anglicise *Ardal.*

Art (m) 'stone' or 'bear'. In England Art is a pet form of *Arthur,* but in Ireland it constitutes a separate name, though it was at times anglicised Arthur. Art McMurrough, the medieval king of Leinster, who bore arms valiantly against the forces of King John, is named Arthur by Froissart. Arthur Griffin (1872-1922), the Nationalist leader, translated his name into Irish as Art.

Artegal (m) A form of *Ardal* used in Spenser's *Faerie Queene* (1590/6).

Arthgallo (m) A form of Ardal which occurs in Geoffrey of Monmouth's *Historia Regum Brittaniae* (1139).

Arthur [*Artúr*] (m) A name of doubtful derivation, perhaps Celtic in origin, or perhaps a Roman sept name, borne by the legendary king of the Britons. The first historical record of the name occurs in the writings of St Adamnan (*c.* 624-704), who mentions an Irishman bearing the name. The name is used in Ireland today. In Irish legend there was an *Artúr,* son of Nemed, who may have been an early Arthur. See also *Atty.*

Ashling {*Aisling*] (f) 'dream', 'vision', 'daydream'. A name originally used in the regions of Derry and Omeath, which is now more widespread. It has sometimes been anglicised as *Esther,* the true Irish form of which is *Eistir.* Today the name is found as *Ashling, Aislinn* and *Aisling. Isleen* is a variant.

Asthore (f) Irish *a stoir,* 'loved one'. A name of Irish derivation listed by Loughead, though it does not seem to be used in Ireland itself.

Attracta [*Athracht*] (f) The name of a Co. Sligo saint. Its use now seems to be declining.

Atty [*Ataigh*] (m) Perhaps a form of *Eochaidh* or possibly a derivative of *ard,* 'high'. This name has been anglicised as *Arthur.*

Audrey (f) Anglo-Saxon, 'noble strength'. An early name revived in England in the present century. Quite widespread in England, it has reached Ireland where it is now fairly well established.

Augusteen (f) An Irish femminine form of *Augustine*.

Augustine [*Agaistin*] (m) Latin 'venerable'. The name of two famous saints, Augustine of Hippo (354-430), author of the *Confessions* and *The City of God,* and Augustine of Canterbury (died *c.* 613). The name has been used quite frequently in Ireland. A feminine *Augusteen* is also found. See also *Austin*.

Auliffe [*Amhlaoibh*] (m) An Irish form of Norse *Olaf,* 'ancestor relics'. Introduced originally by the Norsemen, it was used to replace a native name *Amalgith.* It was sometimes anglicised *Humphrey:* Humphrey O'Sullivan, who kept a diary in Irish, translated his first name as *Amhlaoibh.* There is a church dedicated to St Olaf in Waterford, formerly a Norse city.

Aurnia (f) A variant or equivalent of *Orla,* borne by Aurnia (died 1306), daughter of Donal Og MacCarthy Mor, and wife of Turlogh More O'Brien.

Austin [*Oistin*] (m) A form of *Augustine* which came to be used in England, and presumably spread from there to Ireland. A contemporary Irish example is the singer, Austin Gaffney.

Avril (f) A name of recent origin, coming from French, *Avril.* 'April'. It is increasingly popular in modern Ireland.

Awnan (m) A form of *Adamnan* found at Skreen.

Aylce [*Ailis*] (f) It is not certain whether this name is a variant of *Alice* or a native name; if the latter, it may derive from *ail,* 'noble'.

B

Baethan [*Baothán*] (m) 'little foolish one'. An early name.

Balthasar [*Patifarsa*] (m) Akkadian, 'Bel protect the king'. A name applied by tradition to one of the Magi. It was used in Ireland in the *Nugent* family. Presumably this is the name of Baltazard André Aylmer, Chevalier de St Louis, an Irishman who became a captain in the French Army in 1770. The Gaelic form comes from the Leabhar Breac, a medieval compilation.

Banan (m) Derivative of *ban,* 'white'. Shakespeare's Banquo in *Macbeth* is another derivative of this word.

Banba (f) A name applied to Ireland; it is also the name of an early Irish goddess identified with the country.

Banbhan (m) A diminutive of *banbh,* 'piglet'. An early name.

Barbara [*Bairbre*] (f) Greek, 'strange'. A name used in Ireland both in its own right and to anglicise a native name, *Gormley.*

Barclay (m) A name used as an anglicisation of *Partholon.*

Barnaby [*Barnaib*] (m) An English form of *Barnabas,* meaning uncertain. Barnaby was used in the Castlekevin branch of the *O'Toole* family in the sixteenth and seventeenth centuries. The name has also been used to anglicise *Brian*. The Irish form, *Barnaib*, is taken from the *Martyrology of Gorman*.

Barran (f) 'little top'. The name of an Irish saint.

Barry [*Bearach*] (m) 'spearlike'. St Barry was a disciple of St Kevin and later a missionary in Scotland. Barry is used both as an independent name and as a pet form of *Finbar*, in which case the Irish form is *Barra*. *Bercan* is a diminutive. It is popular today outside Ireland where it may sometimes come from Welsh *ap Harry*, 'son of Harry'.

Bartholomew (m) Hebrew, 'son of Talmai', rendered in Irish as *Pathalón*, and *Bairtliméad*. *Parthalón* (English *Partholon*) is a native name. It is the name of a legendary early settler in Ireland.

Bartley [*Beartlaí*] (m) A variant of *Bartholomew*.

Basil (m) Greek, 'royal'. This name is used in Ireland to anglicise *Brazil*.

Bec [*Beag*] (m) 'small'. The name, or perhaps the nickname, of an early Irish saint known as 'the Prophet'.

Becan [*Beacán*] (m) 'little one'. St Becan founded a monastery in Westmeath in the sixth century.

Beheen [*Baothín*] (m) A diminutive of *baoth*, 'fool'.

Behellagh (m) A variant of *Beolagh*.

Beircheart (m) From Anglo-Saxon, 'bright army'. This name has been variously anglicised as *Benjamin* and *Bernard*.

Benedict (m) Latin, 'blessed'. A name used in Ireland to translate a native name, *Maolbheannachta*, 'hoper for blessing'.

Benen [*Beineon*] (m) An Irish form of the Latin name *Benignus*, 'kind'. *Beanon*, *Beinean* and *Binean* are variants in Irish.

Benjamin (m) Hebrew, 'southerner'. This name is used in Ireland, in Cork, Kerry and Limerick, to anglicise *Beircheart*, itself a name of Anglo-Saxon origin.

Beolagh [*Baothghalach*] (m) 'foolish, valorous'. A name variously rendered in English as *Behellagh*, *Beolagh*, *Boetius* and *Bowes;* and used amongst the *MacEgans*, *O'Dalys*, etc.

Berc(n)an [*Bearchan*] (m) A diminutive of *Barry*. St Bercan is associated with Eigg in Scotland. *Bergin* is a variant.

Berghetta (f) This is the name of the heroine of *Maurice and Berghetta* (1819), anonymously written by William Parnell, Knight of the Shire for Wicklow. The name, which seems to be the author's invention, is perhaps intended to be a form of *Bridget*.

Bergin (m) Variant of *Bercan*.

Berkley (m) This name is used as an anglicisation of *Partholon*.

Bernadette (f) A feminine diminutive of *Bernard*, used in memory of St Bernadette (1844-79), the visionary at Lourdes. It is a popular name in Ireland, but at present it is declining.

Bernard [*Bearnard*] (m) Germanic, 'bear stern'. Bernard is used in Ireland to anglicise *Brian* and *Beircheart* (the latter is itself originally Anglo-Saxon). It persists to this day, but it is growing less popular. *Bernadette* and *Berneen* are feminine forms.

Berneen (f) An Irish diminutive feminine form of *Bernard*. It has the characteristic Irish diminutive suffix -een, representing Gaelic -in.

Betha [*Beatha*] (f) 'life'. A Celtic name, latinised as *Begga*. *Bahee* is a Manx name of similar meaning.

Bidelia (f) A variant of *Bridget,* supposed to be somewhat genteel, and rarely, if ever, used nowadays. It was probably formed by adding the suffix -elia to *Biddy,* a pet form of Bridget.

Bidina (f) Variant of *Bridget*.

Blanche [*Blinne*] (f) French feminine of *blanc,* 'white'. The Irish translation, *Blinne,* is a corruption of *Moninne,* a native Irish name. Neither form is frequently found in Ireland.

Blathmac (m) 'flower son'. The name of a king of Tara who ruled in the first half of the seventh century.

Boetius (m) A name used to anglicise *Beolagh* and *Buagh*.

Bowes (m) A name used to anglicise *Beolagh*.

Boynton (m) A name associated with the Irish River Boyne, where a famous battle of the Jacobite War took place of 1st July 1690.

Bran (m) 'raven'. The name of a Celtic deity, known on both sides of the Irish Sea. His adventures are chronicled in the early Irish literary work, *The Voyage of Bran Son of Febal.* In the *Mabinogion,* a collection of medieval Welsh tales, he appears as *Bendigeidfran* ('blest Bran'), a giant. Bran was also the name of a dog belonging to the legendary hero, Finn MacCool. Woulfe notes the use of the name in the *O'Brien* family. See also *Brandan*.

Brandan (m) Perhaps a derivative of *bran,* 'raven'. St Brandan (*c.* 484-577) was an Irish preacher and abbot.

Branduff [*Brandubh*] (m) 'black raven'. This was the name of a medieval king of Leinster.

Brasil (m) Variant of *Brazil*.

Brazil [*Breasal*] (m) 'strife'. St Brazil (died 801) was a monk of Iona. *Brasil* and *Bresal* are variant forms of this name.

Breeda (f) Variant of *Bridget*.

Brenda (f) In Ireland this is thought of as a feminine form of *Brendan,* but the two names are in fact unconnected. Brenda has its origin in the Shetland Islands, and may mean 'sword'.

Brendan [*Breandan*] (m) 'prince'. A name used in Ireland from early times. St Brendan of Birr (died 571) was called the Chief Prophet of Ireland. St Brendan the Navigator, an Irish saint of the sixth century, made a legendary voyage of which two Latin accounts existed. It has been suggested that he may have journeyed as far as America. His name is often incorrectly rendered *Brandan,* perhaps because of Mount Brandon in Co. Kerry (which was named after him), and possibly because of the Kerry surname *Brandon* (Irish *Mac Breandain,* 'son of Brendan') borne by a branch of the *Fitzmaurice* family. The name is frequently found in Ireland today. It is also used in Britain, and it is very popular in Australia.

Bresal (m) Variant of *Brazil.*

Brian (m) The first part of this name is Celtic and signifies 'hill'. Brian has always been popular in Ireland. It was the name of the most famous of Irish high kings, Brian Boru (reigned 1002-14), the victor of the decisive Battle of Clontarf which put paid to any Norse hopes for the conquest of Ireland. Brian was also the name of the Co. Clare poet, Brian Merriman (*c.* 1757-1808), whose extraordinary work, *Cúirt an Mheadhoin Oidhche* is an early advocation of the emancipation of women. A more recent Irish writer was Brian O'Nolan (1911-66) who wrote under the pseudonyms Flann O'Brien and Myles na Gopaleen.

The name was also known in medieval Brittany, and it was introduced into England from there. The surnames derived from it include *Brian, Brien, Bryan, O'Brien* and *O'Byrne. Bernard* and *Barnaby* were used to anglicise it. The name remains widespread in Ireland. It has been revived in England, and is quite common in the United States and Canada. It is found in Italy as *Briano. Bryan, Brion* and *Bryant* are variants.

Briana (f) A feminine form of *Brian.*

Bride (f) Variant of *Bridget.*

Bridget [*Bríd*] (f) 'high one'. The name of a celebrated Irish saint (*c.*452-523). The English form comes from the Old Irish *Brigit* (hence the modern English form *Brigid),* through Latin *Brigitta* and Old French *Brigette* (modern French *Brigitte).* Bridget was not used in Ireland until the seventeenth century, probably due to reverence for the saint. *Clog Bride,* St Bridget's Bell, said to have been the property of the saint, was exhibited on both sides of the Irish Sea until Henry V put a stop to this practice. The head of St Bridget was supposed to be in Lisbon which resulted in the use of the name in Portugal.

The suggestion that the etymology is the early Irish, *breosaighead,* 'fire arrow' is without foundation. In fact the name is linked with Brigantes, a tribe who inhabited what is now the north of England in early times. There is also a Teutonic name *Bridget* meaning 'mountain protection', borne by a Swedish saint. This name has no relation to the Irish one. *Bre(e)da, Bride* (from which comes the English word *bridewell*), *Bidelia* and *Bidina* are all variants. *Biddy* is a pet form used by Dickens in *Great Expectations* (1860/1).

Brona (f) A derivative of *brón*, 'sorrow', which is occasionally used in modern times.

Brone [*Brón*] (m) 'sorrow'. St Brone was an Irish monk and bishop.

Bryan (m) Variant of *Brian*.

Buagh [*Buach*] (m) 'conqueror'. A name related etymologically to *Boudicca* or *Boadicaea* (died AD 62), queen of the Iceni and leader of a celebrated uprising of the Britons against the Romans in AD 61. *Boetius* and *Victor* have been used to anglicise it.

C

Cadhla (m) 'handsome'. A name used in the Middle Ages. It was borne by the archbishop of Tuam who in 1539 acted as the representative of Rory O'Conor, the last high king of Ireland. In his case it was latinised as *Catholicus*, 'universal'.

Caffar [*Catabharr*] (m) 'helmet'. A name used by the O'Donnells, a family which ruled Tyrconnel, in Co. Donegal, up to the seventeenth century.

Cahal (m) An anglicised spelling of *Cathal*.

Cahir [*Cathaoir*] (m) A name which was once popular in Leinster. *Cathair* was a variant found in a number of families. The name is still used in Ireland today.

Cain [*Cáin*] (m) Hebrew, 'smith'. This name was used to anglicise *Cian*, though why the name of such an unedifying Biblical character should have been chosen is something of a mystery. The use of this name is not confined to Ireland. Dunkling notes that he has traced six bearers of it.

Cairbre (m) 'strong man'. In legend, Cairbre was the first of the Milesians to settle in Ulster. Another legendary Cairbre was said to have defeated the Fianna at the Battle of Gabhra.

Callaghan [*Ceallachán*] (m) A diminutive of *ceallach*, 'strife'. This is normally thought of as a surname though it is also used as a first name. The surname denotes descent from King Callaghan of Munster who ruled in the tenth century. St Callaghan was a monk at Clontibret.

Callough (m) Variant of *Calvagh*.

Calvagh [*Calbhach*] (m) 'bald', cf. Latin *calvinus*. This name, once widespread, is now rare or obsolete. In Irish it was sometimes *An Calbhach*, 'the bald'. *Callough* is a variant. *Charles* was used to anglicise it.

Canice [*Coinneach*] (m) 'comely'. The name of a saint (*c.* 515-599) who founded a monastery at Aghaboe and who gave his name to the city of Kilkenny, in Irish *Cill Coinneach*, 'Canice's church'. The name is in use today. *Kenny* is a variant. *Kenneth* was formerly used to translate it.

Carl (m) A form of *Charles* which occurs in several North

European languages, e.g. German. It is used from time to time in Ireland. Travel, films and literature may all have contributed to its use there. *Karl,* an alternative spelling, is also found.

Carla (f) A feminine form of *Carl,* occasionally used in Ireland.

Carleen (f) An Irish feminine form of *Charles.*

Carmel (f) Hebrew, 'the garden'. A name used in Ireland in honour of Our Lady of Mount Carmel, in the Holy Land. According to legend, the Blessed Virgin was often in the vicinity of this mountain. The Spanish form, *Carmen,* was made well known to opera lovers by Bizet.

Carol (f) A feminine form of *Charles* which is increasingly popular in Ireland.

Caroline (f) A feminine form of *Charles* which is gaining popularity in Ireland.

Carrick [*Carraig*] (m) 'rock'. A name which is found in America and is of Irish derivation; but it is not employed in Ireland itself.

Carroll [*Cearbhall*] (m) 'champion warrior'. A name sometimes anglicised *Charles,* which becomes *Carolus* in Latin. Cearbhall O'Dalaigh (1911-78) was a former President of the Irish Republic.

Carthage [*Carthach*] (m) 'loving'. St Carthage (died 637) was a bishop in Westmeath.

Carthy (m) Variant of *Carthage.*

Cashel [*Caiseal*] (m) An Irish placename meaning 'bulwark', the seat of an archdiocese in Tipperary, and the ancient capital of Munster.

Cashlin [*Caislín*] (m) 'little castle'. A name of Irish derivation, but it does not seem to be used in Ireland itself.

Cathal (m) 'battle mighty'. This was once a common name, and it is still sometimes employed nowadays. Cathal Crobhdhearg, 'Red Hand' (died 1224), was king of Connacht. Modern use of Cathal has been stimulated by the patriot Cathal Brugha (1874-1922), who was killed in the Irish Civil War. *Cathal* is a spelling variant. *Charles* was used as an anglicisation. The Scottish surname *Cadell* is probably derived from Cathal.

Catherine (f) A spelling variant of *Katherine.*

Cathleen (f) A spelling variant of *Kathleen.*

Catriona [*Caitríona*] (f) A Gaelic form of *Katherine,* used by Robert Louis Stevenson in his novel of the same name (1893). The name is at present popular in Ireland.

Cavan (m) An Irish placename used as a first name.

Cecil [*Siseal*] (m) 'little blind one'. The Roman Martyrology mentions a St Cecil, but its use in Ireland, as in England, mainly results from its being the family name of the Marquess of Salisbury.

Cecilia (f) A form of *Cecily* used in Ireland, where it is more common than *Cecily* itself.

Cecily [*Sisile*] (f) A feminine of Cecil. It was introduced into Ireland by the Normans, where it took the Gaelic form *Sile* (English *Sheila*, q.v.). *Sisile* is a later form.

Celia (f) This is probably a form of *Cecily*.

Celsus (m) St Celsus was a bishop of Armagh in the ninth century. Celsus was used to translate his original name *Kellagh*.

Charles [*Séarlas*] (m) Germanic, 'man'. The first Holy Roman Emperor, Charles the Great (*c*. 742-814), was an early bearer of this name. From France it spread, through royal lines, first to Naples, then Hungary, Germany and Spain. It was an unusual name in Ireland until the time of Charles I (1600-49). His father, James I, named him after a later Holy Roman Emperor, Charles V (1500-58). A form of Charles, *Carlus* from Latin *Carolus*, had been previously introduced by the Norsemen. *Searlas* is the Irish language form and, in Hiberno-English, *Charles* is often pronounced with two syllables. It has been used to anglicise a number of native names, particularly *Cathal*, but also *Calvagh, Cormac, Cahir, Carroll, Sorley* and *Turlough*. Charles Stewart Parnell (1846-91) was a famous nineteenth-century politician. Modern Irish examples are Rev. Charles Denis Mary Joseph Anthony O'Conor, claimant to the Irish throne, and Charles Mitchell, a newscaster on Irish television and radio. Feminine forms include *Carleen, Carol, Caroline* and *Charlot(te)*.

Charlot (f) An Irish form of *Charlotte* (Irish, *Searlait)* which is itself a feminine form of *Charles*.

Christian [*Giolla Chríost*] (m, f) The Irish *Giolla Chríost,* 'servant of Christ' was translated into English as Christian, a name which had been in use in England since the twelfth century. Christian is currently increasing in popularity in Ireland. It was originally used as a feminine name, and a modern feminine example has been recorded in Dublin.

Christina [*Chrístíona*] (f) Latin, 'Christian'. Presumably this was introduced into Ireland from England, though the name originally derives from the Continent. It is becoming less popular. *Tina* is a pet form.

Christine [*Cristín*] (f) Another feminine form of *Christian*.

Christopher [*Críostóir*] (m) Greek, 'Christ-bearing'. This name was found in Ireland from the sixteenth century onwards. It is popular today, though not as much as it was formerly. It is often found in its pet form *Christy*. *Chrystal* is a variant.

Chrystal [*Criostal*] (m) A form of *Christopher*. This name gives rise to the Tyrone surname *MacCrystal*.

Cian (m) 'ancient'. An early Irish name which is still in use today. *Kian* and *Kean* are variants. It was occasionally anglicised as *Cain*.

Clare [*Clár*] (f) Latin 'bright'. A name used in Ireland in honour of St Clare of Assisi (1193-1253). The alternative spelling *Claire* is rarely, if ever, found in Ireland. The Irish county of Clare in Munster is unconnected with the name, and seems to derive either from *clar,* 'plain', or from the Anglo-Norman noble family of *de Clare.*

Claudia (f) Latin, perhaps 'lame one'. This name is occasionally found in Ireland. It was probably introduced from England, where it has been in use since at least the sixteenth century.

Clement [*Cléimeans*] (m) Latin, 'merciful'. A name sometimes found in Ireland. The feminine form *Clementina* is no longer used.

Clive (m) A variant of the English word *cliff.* It originally appeared as an English placename, first recorded in 1327, then as a surname. The popularity of the English statesman and founder of the British Empire in India, Robert Clive (1725-74), led to its use as a first name in England. It has spread to Ireland, where it is now occasionally used.

Clodagh (f) The name of a Tipperary river. One of the Marquesses of Waterford seems to have first used this as a first name for his daughter. It is still used in Ireland, and it may have spread overseas because of the popularity of the Irish singer, Clodagh Rogers.

Clotworthy (m) This peculiar name was once considerably used in Ireland. It was probably originally an English surname, transferred to use as a first name. *Tatty* was a common pet form. Clotworthy Rowley was a Member of the Irish Parliament in 1797. The name now seems to have died out.

Cole [*Comhghall*] (m) 'co-pledge'. St Cole was abbot of Bangor in the sixth century.

Colette (f) A feminine diminutive of *Nicholas,* sometimes used in Ireland.

Colin [*Coileán*] (m) 'pup' or 'cub'. A name used from early times. *Coilin* is an Irish variant. It has been latinised as *Caniculus* and *Catulus.* In Ireland the surname *Ó Coileáin,* anglicised as *Collins,* sprang from it. In England the name has two origins: from Scottish Gaelic *Cailean,* and as a diminutive of *Nicholas.* Withycombe mentions an Irish form *Colán,* but there appears to be no evidence for this. Colin is often used in Ireland today.

Colleen [*Cailín*] (f) 'girl'. This is the ordinary Irish word for a girl used as a first name. It is not frequently encountered in Ireland itself, though it is used in other English-speaking countries.

Colm (m) 'dove'. This name represents the Irish form of *Columba.* It is in use today.

Colman [*Colmán*] (m) 'dovelet'. The Irish form of *Columbanus,* which is used quite extensively today. Colman Pearse is a contemporary Irish conductor.

Colmcille (m) 'dove of the church'. The nickname of St Columba.

Columba [*Colm*] (m) Latin, 'dove'. The name of the famous Irish saint (*c.* 521-97) who founded the monastery of Iona and whose biography was written by St Adamnan. His name was given to a well-known public school in Rathfarnham. There was also a female Irish saint called *Columba* (Irish, *Colma).*

Columban (m) A form of *Columbanus.*

Columbanus [*Colmán*] (m) A diminutive of *colm* 'dove'. The name of an Irish missionary saint (*c.* 540-615) who preached on the Continent and founded the monasteries of Luxeuil and Bobbio. He was the author of a monastic rule. Such French surnames as *Colon* and *Coulon,* as well as the Corsican *Colombi,* are possibly derived from this name. So, Yonge tells us, is the German surname *Kohlmann,* but here she is in error – this surname means 'coalman'.

Comyn [*Comán*] (m) 'little wry one'. A name used in both Ireland and Scotland. It is now often a surname.

Conan [*Cónán*] (m) 'small hound'. Conan the Bald, in Irish legend, was one of the Fianna. St Conan of Assaroe (in the present Co. Galway) lived in the sixth century. The name was also known in Brittany: Conan Meriadech was said to be the ancestor of the dukes of that land. The Bretons introduced it into England at the time of the Norman Invasion. It flourished there for centuries and gave rise to a number of surnames. Sir Arthur Conan Doyle (1859-1930), the creator of Sherlock Holmes, was of Irish parentage. In literature, Conan the Cimmerian, a character invented by Robert E. Howard (1906-36), has popularised the name.

Conant (m) Variant of *Conan.*

Concepta (f) A name given in honour of the Immaculate Conception. It is sometimes found in Ireland.

Conchobarre (f) A feminine form of *Connor.*

Congalie (f) A name of uncertain meaning, anglicised as *Constance.*

Conn (m) 'high'. Conn of the Hundred Battles was a legendary Irish monarch. His historicity is doubtful, but he has managed to gain an entry in the *Dictionary of National Biography.* The name Conn is in use in Ireland in modern times. See also *Constantine.*

Connal (f) A name of uncertain meaning, anglicised as *Constance.*

Con(n)or [*Concobhar*] (m) 'hound lover'. An Irish Christian name which gave rise to the surname *O'Con(n)or,* which is one of the most widespread in Ireland today. *Con(n)or* itself is regularly used as a Christian name, but at one time it looked as though it might be replaced by *Cornelius,* which was used to anglicise it. In mythology, Conor mac Nessa was a king of Ulster. Conor Cruise O'Brien is a contemporary statesman and author. Variants are *Conquhare, Constantine, Cornelius, Crogher* and *Crohoore.*

Conchobarre is a feminine form.

Conquhare (m) Variant of *Conor*.

Constance (f) Latin 'constancy'. This was used to anglicise a number of Gaelic names, e.g. the early Irish feminine name *Buan*, which was said to mean 'constancy in goodness'. See also *Congalie, Connal*.

Constantine [*Consaidín*] (m) Latin, 'constant one'. A name used by the *O'Briens* since the twelfth century. It was also used to anglicise *Cuchonnacht* (now obsolete), *Conn* and *Connor*.

Cooey [*Cumhai*] (m) 'hound of the plain'. A Derry name, anglicised as *Quintin*.

Cooley (m) Variant of *Cullo* (now obsolete).

Cormac (m) Perhaps 'raven'. It has had several English variants: *Cormick, Cormock, Cormocke* and *Cormuck*, and it has given rise to the surnames *MacCormack* and *MacCormick*. Cormac mac Art was said to be an ancient king in Irish legend.

Cormac MacCuilleanan was king of Munster and also a bishop. *Kormak* is the Icelandic form of Cormac – the Norse took Irish slaves to Ireland. *Charles* was used to anglicise the name. In literature, Cormac O'Connor Fahy was the hero of *Ninety-Eight* (1897), a novel by John Hill, and Cormac O'Hagan was the hero of the novel *With Poison and Sword* (1910) by W. M. O'Kane.

Cornelius (m) Latin, perhaps 'horned one'. This name was used to anglicise *Connor*. It now seems to be on the wane. Such pseudo-translations *(Jeremiah* is another example) are now considered old-fashioned.

Covey [*Cúmhéa*] (m) 'hound of Meath'. A name used by the *MacNamaras*.

Crevan [*Criomhthann*] (m) 'fox'. A name which seems to have been used chiefly in Leinster.

Crogher (m) A variant of *Conor*, once used in north-eastern Ireland.

Crohoore (m) A variant of *Conor*, once used in north-eastern Ireland. Pronunciation in modern Gaelic of *Conchobhar*, Irish for Conor, is the same as Crohoore.

Cronan [*Crónán*] (m) 'little dark-brown one'. St Cronan founded the monastery of Roscrea in the seventh century. He became its first abbot. The name is rarely if ever used nowadays.

Cuchulainn (m) 'hound of Culann'. The name, or rather, the nickname, of the greatest hero of Irish mythology. His real name was *Setanta,* and he obtained the name Cuchulainn by slaying the ferocious hound of Culann and afterwards volunteering to take on the dead creature's duties. He defended Ulster against the forces of Queen Maeve of Connacht, and his exploits are recorded in the epic *Táin Bó Cuailgne*.

Cumania [*Cuman*] (f) The name of a sixth-century Irish

saint, said to have been the sister of St Colmcille.

Cyril [*Coireall*] (m) Greek, 'lordly'. A name used in Ireland to anglicise *Kerill*.

D

Dagda [*Daghda*] (m) 'the good god'. This was the name of an important deity of the pagan Irish. According to medieval legend, he was the leader of the Tuatha De Danaan, the traditional early inhabitants of Ireland. Loughead notes Dagda as a given name.

Dahy [*Dáithí*] (m) 'speed', 'agility'. The name of a king of Tara, ancestor of the *O'Dowds*, who, according to legend, raided continental Europe and was struck by lightning at the foot of the Alps. Dahy has often been anglicised as *David*, and it is common as an Irish 'translation' of that name. *Nathy*, the name of an Irish saint, is possibly a variant.

Daireen (f) This name was first used by the Limerick author, F. Frankfort Moore, for the heroine of his novel *Daireen* (1893). It appears to be the author's invention.

Dallan (m) A diminutive of *dall*, 'blind'. St Dallan (died 598) was a bishop of Donaghmore.

Damien (m) A French form of *Damian* (Irish, *Daman*) which perhaps is connected with a Greek word meaning 'to tame'. *Damien* is now quite popular in Ireland.

Dana (f, m) Dana was an important Irish pagan goddess who gave her name to the Tuatha De Danaan, the legendary inhabitants of Ireland. It is also the name of a popular Irish singer, but in her case the name derives from *dana*, 'bold'. There is a masculine name *Dana* which is Teutonic and signifies 'Dane'; this name is borne by the contemporary actor, Dana Andrews.

Daniel (m) Hebrew, 'God is my judge'. A popular name in Ireland. It was used to anglicise the common native name *Donal*, and so it became well established. The Irish forms are *Dainéal* and *Dainial*. Daniel O'Connell (1775-1847), a major Irish political figure in the nineteenth century who secured Catholic Emancipation, further popularised the name. So Irish a name has Daniel become that Spike Milligan used it as the name of the protagonist of his hilarious Irish novel, *Puckoon* (1963).

Darby (m) A form of *Dermot* which occurred in Limerick and Tipperary. It had spread from Ireland to England as early as 1560. Henriette Templeton used the name in her novel *Darby O'Gill and the Good People* which was filmed by Walt Disney as *Darby O'Gill and the Little People*. Darby O'Drive was also a character in William Carleton's novel *Valentine McClutchey* (1845).

Darcy (m) A branch of the *Darcy* family – whose surname comes either from the placename of Arcy-Ste-Restitue or that of Arcy-sur-Cure – came to Ireland in the fourteenth century, and the surname was adopted as a Christian name there.

Darerca (f) The name of a saint associated with Valentia Island who, according to tradition, was the sister of St Patrick. Legend credits her with nineteen children.

Darkey [*Dorchaidhe*] (m) The English form of this name is unusual. *Darcy* has often been substituted for it.

Darragh (m) A name connected in meaning with *dair*, 'oak'. It has been used from time to time in Ireland in modern times, but it is now on the increase.

Darren (m) A name of obscure origin, said to be Irish. It is used in Ireland today. There is a character called Darren in the American television series *Bewitched*, first shown in the 1960s. It is almost certain that this series contributed to the name's recent popularity. According to Rule, it means 'little great one'.

David [*Dáivi*] (m) A Hebrew name of uncertain meaning, once thought to signify 'loved one'. It was used as an equivalent of *Daithi* in Ireland and *Dewi* in Wales, the latter being the real name of St David of Menevia. *Dáibhidh* was a form borne by the eighteenth-century poet O'Bruadair, and *Daibheid* was a form taken from Norman French *Davet* (a diminutive). David is increasingly popular in Ireland today.

Dawn (f) This name, unused before the present century, occurs occasionally in Ireland.

Dé (m) A translation of *Mogue*, used also in Brittany, where it is the name of the village of St Dé.

Deborah (f) Hebrew 'bee'; later, 'eloquence'. A Biblical name adopted by the English Puritans. It was brought to Ireland from England and was used to anglicise the native name, *Gobinet*. It is popular in Ireland today.

Decla (f) An unusual feminine form of *Declan*.

Declan [*Deaglán*] (m) The name of an early Irish saint, which has noticeably increased in popularity in modern times.

Deirdre (f) A name of uncertain meaning, perhaps signifying 'fear', perhaps 'one who rages', or perhaps 'broken-hearted one'. It was borne by the heroine of a tragic Irish legend. Deirdre, the betrothed of the king of Ulster, eloped with one of the three sons of Uisneach. All three sons were slain by the king, and Deirdre was left to mourne them. Two prominent Irish writers have used this legend: W. B. Yeats in his *Deirdre* (1907), and J. M. Synge in his *Deirdre of the Sorrows* (1910). It was the name of a character with second sight in Nicholas Stewart Grey's excellent children's novel, *Down in the Cellar* (1961). It is popular in Ireland today.

Denis (m) The Greek god of wine was Dionysus, and the name *Dionysius*, 'servant of Dionysus', was used in early times. Denis – sometimes spelt *Dennis* or *Denys* – is a shortened form of this. In Ireland Denis was used to anglicise *Donagh* which established the name. However its popularity has sharply decreased in recent times.

Denise (f) A feminine form of *Denis*, originally from France, but presumably imported into Ireland from England in modern times. The name is now well established in Ireland.

Derek (m) Germanic, 'people ruler'. This is a form of the name *Theodoric*. Old French *Terrick*, Dutch *Dirk* and English *Derrick* are related forms. Derek was introduced into England by Flemings and it occurs there from the fifteenth century onwards. It has been revived in England in modern times and has spread to Ireland, where it is now quite common.

Derforgal (f) This is a variant of a native name, *Dervorgilla*.

Dermitius (m) A latinised form of *Dermot* occasionally recorded, e.g., there was a Captain Dermitius Coghlan, of King's County and Tipperary, a soldier of the Commonwealth.

Dermod (m) Variant of *Dermot*.

Dermot [*Diarmuid*] (m) 'envy free'. The name of an important hero of Irish legend, who eloped with Grania, the betrothed of Finn MacCool. Dermot MacMurrough was the king of Leinster who invited the Normans into Ireland in the twelfth century. *Darby* was a form of Dermot used in Limerick and Tipperary; *Jarmy* was used by the *O'Kanes* and the *O'Mullans*. It was anglicised as *Jeremiah* in Cork and Kerry, and it has also been anglicised *Jerome* and *Edward*. Dermot is quite popular in Ireland today. *Diarmis* may be a variant. See also *Dermitius, Dermod* and *Kermit*.

Dervla (f) A name used to translate Irish *Dearbhail*, 'true desire'; *Derval* and *Dervilia* are also translations of this name. Dervla Murphy is a contemporary Irish writer and traveller.

Desmond [*Deasún*] (m) An Irish placename, 'South Munster' (i.e. Cork and Kerry), and not, as may be supposed, from Thomond, North Munster. It was first transferred to use as a surname, and then came into use as a first name. It is found frequently today.

Devnet (f) A form of *Dympna*.

Dichu (m) 'great hound'. St Dichu was said to have been the first Irish convert to Christianity made by St Patrick.

Doctor (m) Dunkling says there is an Irish custom of giving this name to the seventh son of a seventh son, but it has not been possible to verify this. However, in Irish folklore, such a person is said to have healing powers.

Dolores (f) Spanish, 'sorrows'. This name is given in honour of the Blessed Virgin who is sometimes referred to as *Maria de los Dolores*, 'Mary of the Sorrows'. The name used to be confined almost exclusively to Catholics but this is no longer the case. It is occasionally used in Ireland today.

Dominic [*Doiminic*] (m) Latin, 'of the Lord'. A name used in Ireland in honour of St Dominic de Guzman (1170-1221). Two unusual Irish forms were *Damhlaic* and *Damhnaic*. The spelling *Dominick* is often used.

Dominica (f) Feminine form of *Dominic*. St Dominica, an early Irish saint, was martyred in Germany.

Donagh [*Donnchadh*] (m) 'brown warrior'. This is a common Irish name, borne by the High King Donagh (died 1064), son of Brian Boru. It has sometimes been anglicised as *Denis* or *Donat*. *Duncan* was originally a pet form of this name. Donagh O'Malley was a twentieth-century Irish politician.

Donal [*Dónal*] (m) 'world mighty'. A name frequently employed in Ireland, though at one stage it was commonly anglicised as *Daniel*. In Scotland, the Gaelic equivalent, *Domhnall*, has been translated into English as *Donald*. The *O'Donnells* and *MacDonnells* or *MacDonalds* all take their names from *Donal*. Donal of Bangor was an Irish saint.

Donat (m) Latin, 'given'. This was used to translate the native name *Donagh*. St *Donatus* (the Latin form) was said to have been an Irishman. *Donato*, the Italian form, has been noted amongst the Italian community in Ireland.

Donegal (m) The name of an Irish town and county, used as a personal name. In Irish it becomes *Dún na nGall*, which means 'fort of the foreigners'.

Donelle (f) The feminine form of *Donal*.

Donleavy [*Donn Sléibhe*] (m) 'brown of the hill'. A once-popular name, from which the surnames *Donleavy* and *Dunlop* sprang. It was also used in Scotland, where the strange form *Downsleif* is recorded.

Donn (m) 'brown'. This rare name was chiefly used by the *Maguires*.

Doon (f) The Hill of Doon in Lough Mask has provided this unusual first name.

Doreen [*Doireann*] (f) This is perhaps an Irish form of *Dorothy* (Greek, 'God's gift') or a form of the native name *Dorren*, 'sullen'. It was used in Edna Lyall's novel *Doreen* (1894). *Dorothy* itself is sometimes used in Ireland.

D'Orsay (m) An anglicisation of the Irish name *Dorchaidhe*.

Dougal [*Dúghall*] (m) 'dark foreigner'. This Gaelic name is primarily used in Scotland. It is the name of a remarkable dog in the television series, *The Magic Roundabout*.

Douglas [*Dúghlas*] (m) 'black blue'. Douglas is mainly used in Scotland, though it also occurs in Ireland. Douglas Hyde (1860-1949) was the first President of Ireland (1938-45).

Dowle (m) An unusual form of *Donal*, borne by a member of the *Barry* family of Sandville, Co. Limerick, who died in 1640.

Downett (f) A form of *Dympna*.

Doyle (m) This surname derives from *Dubhghall*, 'dark foreigner', indicating Scandinavian ancestry. Doyle may also indicate ancestry springing from the French towns, Oyle or Ouilly. It has come to be used as a first name.

Duald [*Dualtach*] (m) 'black-jointed'. A name borne by the writer, Dubhaltach MacFirbisigh (1580-1660). It was sometimes anglicised *Dudley*.

Dualtagh (m) Variant of *Duald*.

Dubhdara (m) 'black (man) of the oak'. A West Connacht name.

Dubside [*Dubh Sithe*] (m) 'black of peace'. An early name, borne by a Rector of Iona in the twelfth century.

Dudley (m) Originally this was a surname coming from Dudley in Worcestershire. It became a first name in the nineteenth century, and was used in Ireland to anglicise *Duald, Dubhdaleithe* ('black man of the two sides') and *Dubhdara*. It continues in use.

Duff [*Dubh*] (m) 'black'; when used of a man, it means 'black-haired'.

Duvessa [*Dubheasa*] (f) 'dark beauty'. A name used in Ireland in the Middle Ages. The death of one Duvessa O'Farrell was recorded in 1301.

Dwyer (m) An Irish surname which has been recorded as a Christian name in Northern Ireland.

Dymphna (f) Variant of *Dympna*.

Dympna [*Damhnait*] (f) A name perhaps meaning 'befitted'. St Dympna of Tedavnat was an early Irish saint. Another St Dympna of Gheel in Belgium may have been Irish. Both *Dympna* and its variant *Dymphna* are in use today. *Devnet* is another variant.

E

Ea (m) Variant of *Aodh*.

Eachann (m) 'horse lord'. This name was exported to Scotland, where it was anglicised as *Hector* (Irish *Eachtar*), which may mean 'holding fast'.

Ealga (f) 'noble'. Ireland is sometimes referred to as *Inis Ealga*, 'the Noble Isle', which is the source of this unusual name.

Eamon(n) (m) This is the Irish form of *Edmund*, Anglo-Saxon, 'rich protection'; but the name is now frequently used to translate *Edward*. Eamon De Valera (1882-1975) was an important Irish politician and president. Eamon Andrews is a present-day television compere. The name is currently quite popular. *Aimon* was a spelling variant which no longer seems to be used. *Iamonn* was another variant used in Derry and Omeath.

Eavan [*Aoibheann*] (f) 'fair form'. A name used in early times which has been revived. Eavan Boland is a contemporary Irish poetess.

Echlin [*Eaclain*] (m) A name used by the *O'Kanes* of Derry. See also *Aichlinn*.

Edana (f) A feminine of *Aidan*.

Edith (f) Anglo-Saxon, 'happy war'. This name has occasionally been used in Ireland. *Editha*, probably a variant, occurs in the *Wallis* family.

Edmund (m) In Ireland this name is usually represented by

Eamonn, but is sometimes bestowed in its own right. Recently the spelling *Edmond* has become more popular. C. S. Lewis (1898-1963) the Northern-Irish writer, has an Edmund in his Narnian chronicles.

Edward (m) Anglo-Saxon, 'rich guard'. The true Irish form of this name is *Eadbhard*, but this has been largely replaced by *Eamonn*. Edward was introduced after the Norman Invasion (1169). Recently it has sharply declined in popularity.

Egan [*Aodhgan*] (m) 'little fire'. Egan O'Rahilly was an Irish language poet in the seventeenth century. Egan is common nowadays as a surname.

Eileen [*Eibhlin*] (f) This is probably an elaboration of *Evelyn*, rather than a form of *Helen*, as is sometimes supposed. *Eily* is a pet form. The name is frequently encountered in Ireland today, and it has spread abroad. It became common in England and Wales from about the 1920s onwards. A variant, *Aileen*, is sometimes found.

Eilis [*Eilís*] (f) The Irish form of *Elizabeth*. *Eilise* is a variant. It was used, on occasion, to translate *Alice*, *Alicia* and *Letitia* – names wholly unrelated to it. Eilis Dillon is a modern Irish authoress.

Eimar (m) This name has come into use in Ireland in modern times. Its origin is obscure, but, as it does not appear to be used anywhere else, it is presumably Irish. It is unlikely to be connected with Irish *eimh*, 'swift', or with the Germanic name *Einar*, 'chief'.

Elaine (f) A form of *Helen* used in Arthurian romance. Tennyson's *Idylls of the King* (1859-88) led to its modern use, and it is now an established name in Ireland.

Elan (f) This is perhaps a form of *Helen* which is used in Ireland. It was borne by a daughter of Teague O'Meara, of Lismisk, Co. Tipperary, who died in 1636.

Eleanor [*Eileanóir*] (f) The name *Helen* became *Alienor* in Provençal, and this, in turn, was transformed into Eleanor. It became popular in England in Norman times due to Queen Eleanor, wife of Edward I. The Normans brought the name to Ireland. *Eleanora* (Irish *Eilíonóra)* is a variant. Another version perhaps occurs in the name of the Irish martyr, St *Ealanor*.

Elhe [*Ele*] (m) 'bier', 'litter'. The name of the legendary ancestor of the *Healy* family.

Eliza (f) A form of *Elizabeth*, which once enjoyed considerable popularity in Ireland.

Elizabeth [*Eilís*] (f) Hebrew, 'my God is satisfaction'. In the New Testament, St Elizabeth was the mother of John the Baptist. The name was used in the Middle Ages chiefly in honour of St Elizabeth of Hungary (1207-31). It probably first reached Ireland in the variant form of *Isabel*. Elizabeth became extremely popular in Ireland, as well as in England, Wales and Scotland, but its use has sharply declined in modern times. *Beth*, *Liz*, *Lizzie*, *Elsie*, and *Lilibet* are all used as pet forms. *Elisa*, *Elsa* and *Elspeth* are variants.

Ellen (f) A form of *Helen* which became fashionable in Ireland round about the middle of the century, but between 1950 and 1970 it fell rapidly from favour.

Elli (m) Variant of *Ailbe* (see *Alby*).

Elly (m) Variant of *Ailbe* (see *Alby*).

Elva [*Ailbhe*] (f) A name sometimes anglicised *Olive*. *Alvy* is an English variant, *Oilbhe* an Irish one.

Emer [*Eimhear*] (f) Emer was the wife of the hero, Cuchulainn, in Irish legend. It has come into use in modern times, no doubt due to the Gaelic Revival and perhaps because of W. B. Yeats' play, *The Only Jealousy of Emer* (1921).

Emily [*Eimile*] (f) The feminine form of a Roman clan name, *Aemilius*, which was to some degree confused with *Amelia*, a different name of Germanic origin. Emily was presumably imported from Britain.

Emma (f) Germanic, 'universal'. This name, much used in England and Wales, is quite popular in Ireland today.

Emmet (m) This was the surname of the renowned eighteenth-century rebel, Robert Emmet. It is sometimes conferred by modern Irish parents on their sons in commemoration of the patriot.

Ena (f) A form of *Ethna*.

Enda [*Éanna*] (m) Perhaps a derivation of *éan*, 'bird', meaning 'birdlike', 'avian'. St Enda (died *c.* 590), one of the most famous Irish saints, is associated with the Aran Islands. The name is in use in modern times.

Eneas (m) A variant of *Aeneas* which has been used to translate Gaelic *Eigneachan* (see *Ignatius*).

Ennis [*Inis*] (f) The name of the capital of Co. Clare, used as a first name.

Eochaidh (m) Because it is so difficult for English speakers to pronounce, this name has declined from the position of popularity it once held in Ireland. There are several more pronounceable variants (e.g. *Achaius*, *Aghy*, *Atty*, *Eoi*, *Oho*, *Ogh(i)e*, *Syka*) which are listed separately. The Latin form, *Equitius*, has been recorded as an independent name.

Eoghan (m) 'well born'. This Celtic name is etymologically identical with Greek *Eugene*, and is often used to translate it. The Welsh name *Eugeuin*, translated into English as *Owen*, has the same meaning – and indeed, in Ireland Owen is sometimes used to translate Eoghan. Eoghan has been translated as *John* in Omeath, due to confusion with *Eoin*. The Scottish *Ewen* may be a form of this name.

Eoi (m) Variant of *Eochaidh*.

Eoin (m) An Irish form of *John*, presumably from Latin *Johannes*. It is probably closely related to Scottish Gaelic *Iain*. Eoin still survives in modern Ireland, but more and more it is being replaced by *Sean* from Norman French

Jehan which was introduced after the Norman Invasion of 1169, and by the English name *John* itself.

Erc [*Earc*] (m) 'red' or 'speckled'. This name was once frequently found in Munster, but it has now disappeared.

Eric (m) A Germanic name of uncertain meaning, which was revived in England in the nineteenth century. It has occasionally been used in modern Ireland.

Erin(a) (f) The Irish word for Ireland, used as a Christian name. It is employed in the United States, Canada and Australia, but it is not used in Ireland at all.

Ernan [*Earnán*] (m) 'little-experienced one'. This name is used in Ireland as an equivalent of *Ernest*.

Ernest (m) Germanic, 'vigour'. A name used in Ireland to anglicise *Ernan*.

Esther [*Eistir*] (f) A Persian name of unknown meaning, which was used in Ireland to 'translate' *Ashling*. There was an Irish custom of conferring this name on children born at Easter.

Etain (f) According to Irish legend, Etain was the lover of the fairy man, Midir. *Aideen* is a variant. The name was probably made popular by *The Immortal Hour* (1914), an opera by Rutland Boughton based on the legend.

Eth (m) Variant of *Aodh*.

Ethna [*Eithne*] (f) A feminine form of *Aidan*. *Annie* was used to anglicise it – which at one time resulted in Annie being extremely popular, much more so than *Ann(e)*. Annie is less popular now than it was at the turn of the century; but *Eithne/Ethna* has been revived in modern times. *Ena* and *Etney* are variants.

Etney (f) Variant of *Ethna*.

Eugene (m) Greek, 'well born'. A name used to translate *Eoghan*.

Eunan (m) Variant of *Adamnan*.

Eustace [*Iustas*] (m) Greek, possibly 'fruitful'. A name introduced into Ireland after the Norman Invasion. Since then it has occasionally been used. It was equated with *Iusdas*, a native name for which O'Hart gives the unlikely etymology of 'knowledge desk'.

Eva [*Aoife*] (f) The Latin form of *Eve*. It was used to translate Irish *Aoife*, a name found in legend. It was also the name of the daughter of King Dermot of Leinster, who married Strongbow, the leader of the Norman Invasion. Eva Gore Booth (1870-1926) was an Irish poetess. *Aoife* has become popular in modern times.

Eve [*Éabha*] (f) Perhaps Hebrew, 'lively'. It is not a common name in Ireland.

Eveleen (f) An Irish diminutive of *Eva*.

Evelyn (m, f) A Germanic name, occasionally used in Ireland.

F

Fachnan [*Fachtna*] (m) The name of a sixth-century Irish saint and first bishop of Ros Carbery. *Festus* has been used to anglicise this name; *Faughnan* is a variant.

Fardoragh [*Feardorcha*] (m) 'dark man'. A name which was – fairly popular in the sixteenth century. It was anglicised both as *Frederick* and *Ferdinand*.

Farghy (m) Variant of *Fergus*, perhaps now obsolete.

Farrell (m) Variant of *Fergal*.

Farry [*Fearadhach*] (m) 'manly'. This name was widespread in early times. It has been anglicised as *Ferdinand*.

Faughnan (m) Variant of *Fachnan*.

Feary (m) A form of *Fiachra*.

Fe(c)hin [*Feichin*] (m) 'little raven'. The name of an Irish saint. It was anglicised as *Festus*.

Felim(id) [*Feilim*] (m) 'ever good'. Felim was king of Connacht in the Middle Ages. The Spanish form of the name is *Felime*. Attempts to anglicise it as *Felix* and *Philip* have proved successful, as the name is rarely encountered today. *Phelim(y)* is an alternative spelling.

Felimy (m) Variant of *Felimid*.

Felix (m) Latin, 'happy'. This name was used to anglicise *Felim*, *Phelim* and *Felimid*; e.g. Sir Phelim O'Neill, executed by the English in the seventeenth century, changed his name to *Felix*.

Fenella (f) The Scottish form of *Finola* which is occasionally found in Ireland.

Feories (m) A name which now seems to be obsolete. It is a variant of *Pierce*, presumably from the Irish *Piaras*.

Ferdinand (m) Germanic, 'journey risk'. This name was used in Ireland to anglicise *Farry, Fardoragh, Fergananym,* and *Fergus*.

Fergal [*Fearghall*] (m) 'man of strength'. St Fergal (died 784) was an Irish saint associated with Salzburg, whose name was latinised as *Virgil*. Fergal is still used today. *Farrell* and *Forgael* are variants.

Fergananym [*Fearganainm*] (m) 'nameless man'. This curious name, sometimes anglicised as *Ferdinand,* used to be fairly popular in Ireland. It may sometimes have been applied to unbaptised persons.

Fergus [*Fearghus*] (m) 'man vigour'. An early Gaelic name, still closely associated with Ireland and Scotland. Fergus mac Erca was said to have led the Gaels from Ireland to Scotland in the fifth century. In the eighth century another Irishman, St Fergus, was a bishop in Scotland. *Forcus* was the Pictish equivalent. Later when Irish names were anglicised, Fergus was 'translated' as *Ferdinand* by the wealthy, *Fardy* by those who were not so well-to-do. *Farghy* is a variant noted by Yonge, who also mentions a feminine form, *Fergusiana*. The name continues in use in Ireland, Scotland and even northern England.

Festus (m) This rather strange, Latin name was used to 'translate' *Fachan* and *Fehin*.

ffranck (m) This was used as a middle name in the family of *Rolleston* of ffranckfort and Sandbrook. The double *f* in medieval times was a way of rendering a capital *F*. The earliest traced bearer was James ffranck Rolleston (born 1742).

Fiach (m) 'raven'. Two Irish words for raven, *bran* and *fiach,* were used a Christian names. In the sixteenth century Fiach MacHugh O'Beirne joined forces against the English with Red Hugh O'Donnell after his escape from Dublin Castle.

Fiachra (m) Perhaps a derivative of *fiach*, 'raven'. St Fiacre (died *c.* 670) was said to have been an Irishman, and this may have been his original name. His name was eventually used for a type of coach in Paris. *Feary* is a variant of Fiachra. Macpherson's Fiachere, son of Fingal, may be derived from this name.

Fidelma [*Fideilme*] (f) A name which is quite widespread in modern Ireland. Fidelma Murphy is a contemporary actress.

Finbar [*Fionnbhárr*] (m) 'fair top' or 'fair head'. St Finbar (*c.* 470-548) established a monastery in the south of Ireland, where the City of Cork now stands. The name is still used in Ireland today, e.g. Finbar Nolan is a modern faith healer. *Barry* (Irish *Barra)* is a pet form.

Fineen [*Finín*] (m) 'fair offspring'. A name particularly associated with West Munster. It has been anglicised as *Florence*. *Fineen* is a spelling variant.

Finella (f) Variant of *Finola*.

Fingal (m) A corruption of Irish *Finn* which originated in Scotland and has been made well known by Macpherson's Ossianic poems (1795) and Mendelssohn's *Fingal's Cave* (1830). Fingal occurs as early as the fourteenth century in the works of the Scottish poet, John Barbour (*c.* 1316-95).

Fingar (m) A name formed from *fionn* 'fair-haired.' It is the name of a fifth-century Irish saint.

Fin(n)ian (m) A name formed from *Fionn* 'fair'. St Finian founded the abbey of Moville in the sixth century.

Finlugh [*Fionnlugh*] (m) 'fair winning'. The name of an Irish saint who was a missionary in Scotland in the sixth century. He returned to Ireland to become an abbot.

Finn [*Fionn*] (m) 'fair'. Also *Fynn*. This is the name of one of the great heroes of Irish mythology, Finn MacCool. Mythologists have suggested that he was an aspect of the god Lugh, and that even a place as far away as Vienna (Latin *Vindobona)*derives its name from him. He was the leader of the Fianna, the father of the master-poet Ossian, and the pursuer of Dermot. In folklore Finn was depicted as a giant, but in myth he was of normal stature. He is said to have erected the Giants' Causeway on the Antrim coast.

There is also a Germanic name *Finn*, which Yonge connects with the Irish name, but which probably has an entirely different origin and means 'wise as a Finn' – in the middle ages the Finns were famous for sorcery. *Finni* and *Finnr*, used in medieval Iceland, may come from the Irish Finn. See also *Fingal*.

Finna (f) A name used in medieval Iceland. It is perhaps derived from Irish *fionn*, 'fair'.

Finola [*Fionnuala*] (f) A well-known Irish name, frequently seen nowadays in its shortened form *Nuala*. *Finella* and *Fynballa* are variants. It was 'translated' as *Flora* or *Penelope*. *Fenella* is the form used in Scotland.

Fintan [*Fionntán*] (m) 'little fair one'. St Fintan was a sixth-century abbot of Clonenagh. The name is used in modern times.

Fiona [*Fióna*] (f) This Scottish name was invented in the nineteenth century by the writer, William Sharp, who used it for his pseudonym 'Fiona Macleod'. It comes from Gaelic *fionn*, 'fair'. It has spread from Scotland, becoming particularly popular in Northern Ireland. It is also often found in the Republic.

Fitzgerald [*MacGerailt*] (m) Norman French, 'son of *Gerald*'. The prefix Fitz- is cognate with the modern French *fils*, and readily translated into Irish as Mac. *Fitzgerald* was the name of a prominent Norman noble family in the Middle Ages, a family which included the Earls of Kildare. It is now sometimes used as a first name.

Fitzgibbon (m) A surname used as a first name. It means 'son of *Gibbon*'. (a form of *Gilbert*).

Fitzjames (m) 'son of James'. This name was borne by the Limerick writer Fitz-james O'Brien (1828-62) who emigrated to the United States and was killed in the American Civil War.

Flann (m) 'blood-red', 'red-wat'. An early name which was once quite widespread. It was anglicised as *Florence*. Flann O'Brien was a pen-name used by Brian O'Nolan (1911-66).

Flannan (m) A diminutive of *Flann*, still in use today, but growing less popular.

Flora (f) Latin, derivative of *flos*, 'flower'. Flora was used to translate the Irish name *Blath*, 'flower'. It was also used to translate *Finola*.

Florence (m, f) Latin, 'flowering one'. Florence was once used as a masculine name in England as well as in Ireland; however, its use for boys in England was rare after the seventeenth century. In Ireland its use as a masculine name has persisted, mainly because it was employed to anglicise names such as *Fineen*, *Fitheal* and *Flann*. *Flor*, *Florrie* and *Flurry* are pet forms. As a feminine name it is used to translate *Blathnaid*, derived from *blath*, 'flower'.

Forgael (m) Variant of *Fergal*.

Frances [*Proinséas*] (f) The feminine form of *Francis*, occurring in the latter half of the thirteenth century as Italian *Francesca,* and French *Françoise.* It spread to Ireland where it was once popular, but it has now gone out of fashion. The pet form *Fanny,* occasionally given as an independent name, was used to anglicise the native name *Fainche.*

Francis [*Proinsias*] (m) Italian, *Francesco,* 'Frenchman'. This nickname was given to St Francis of Assisi (1182-1226) who made the name well known throughout Europe. It became widespread in Ireland, as in other countries, but it is less used today.

Frederick (m) Germanic, 'peace ruler'. This name was used in Ireland to anglicise *Fardoragh.*

Fursey [*Fursa*] (m) According to legend St Fursey had a vision of the world to come. His name was used by Mervyn Wall (1908–) in a number of amusing satirical novels.

Fynballa (f) A variant of *Finola.*

Fynn (m) A spelling variant of *Finn.*

G

Gabriel [*Gaibrial*] (m) Hebrew, 'strong man of God'. A name used from time to time in Ireland, e.g. in 1754 an Irishman, Gabriel Redmond, Chevalier de St Louis, became a captain in the French army. The modern-day television compère, *Gay* Byrne has an unusual pet form of this name.

Gael (m) According to medieval Irish legend, this is the name of the hero from whom the Irish race took its name. In fact, the word *Gael* (Old Irish, *Goidel)* is derived from Welsh *Gwyddyl. Gathelus* is a variant.

Gale [*Gál*] (m) Various derivations have been given for this name, e.g., Irish 'vapour'; Germanic, 'song'; Danish, 'crow'; and Icelandic, 'furious'.

Gall (m) Perhaps 'rooster'. St Gall (*c.* 550-640) was a follower of St Columbanus. He settled in Switzerland, where the town and canton of Sankt-Gallen were named after him.

Galvin (m) This name is derived either from *gealbhan,* 'bright white', or from *gealbhan,* 'sparrow'.

Gareth [*Gairiad*] (m) In Arthurian romance, Gareth was a brother of Sir Gawaine. The Irish form occurs in the *Lorgaireacht an tSoidigh Naomhtha,* an Irish rendering of a version of the Grail legend. It may derive from a Welsh name or be a form of *Gerald.* The use of Gareth in England in the nineteenth century probably owes much to Tennyson's *Idylls of the King* (1859-88). It is occasionally used in Ireland, where it probably spread from England.

Garrett [*Gearóid*] (m) The name *Gerlad* became *Gearoid* or *Gioroid* in Irish, and was then anglicised as *Garrett* (a name which has no connection with *Gareth).* Garret is one of the more popular Irish names today. The combination *Garrett-Michael* was used on a number of occasions in the

O'Byrne family.

Gary (m) This is perhaps a form of *Gerald*. It has been used from time to time in Ireland. In the 1930s the American film actor, Gary Cooper, made the name a popular one.

Gaspar (m) A form of *Jasper* occasionally used in Ireland.

Gathelus (m) Variant of *Gael*.

Gavin (m) This name, frequently used in Scotland, but more rarely in Ireland, may come from Teutonic *Gavja*, 'district', or from Welsh *Gwalchmai,* 'May hawk'. It occurs as *Gauvain* in French and *Gawain* in English Arthurian romance.

Gemma (f) Italian (f) Italian, 'gem'. A name used in Ireland to commemorate St Gemma Galgani (died 1903). Gemma Craven is a contemporary Irish actress.

Geoffrey [*Seathrún*] (m) This name is Germanic, but it has varying origins, meaning both 'district peace' and 'pledge peace'. The name is sometimes confused with *Godfrey*, to which it is unrelated. The French *Geoffroi* and *Jeoffroi*, Breton *Jaffrez*, became in English Geoffrey and *Jeffrey*. In Ireland, where the name was probably introduced after the Norman Invasion, a variety of forms grew up: *Seafra, Seafraid, Seartha, Searthra,* and *Siofrai* (from Geoffrey) and *Seathrun* (from a French diminutive of the name). Seathrún Céitinn (in English, Geoffrey Keating) was a priest of the Cromwellian period who wrote a history of Ireland entitled *Foras Feasa ar Éirinn.*

Some of these Gaelic forms have been re-anglicised as *Sheary* and *Sheron.* Geoffrey continues to be used in Ireland today.

George [*Seoirse*] (m) Greek, 'farmer'. The name of the patron saint of England, whose cult was introduced by returning crusaders. George was used by the royal House of Hanover in the eighteenth century, and it came into general use in Ireland at that time. It is now established, though it appears to be less used today. The Portuguese form *Jorge* is borne by Jorge The O'Neill of Clanaboy, claimant to the Irish throne.

Georgina (f) A feminine form of *George,* sometimes found in Ireland.

Gerald [*Gearalt*] (m) Germanic, 'spear rule'. This was introduced to Ireland after the Norman Invasion, but it has tended to give way to *Garrett*. It has also been confused with *Gerard* in both Ireland and Wales. *Gary* is possibly a variant.

Geraldine [*Gearóidín*] (f) The *Fitzgeralds,* earls of Kildare, were known as the *Geraldines,* and in the sixteenth century the poet Surrey saluted Lady Elizabeth Fitzgerald as 'the Fair Geraldine' which possibly started the name. Its popularity may have been increased by its use in Coleridge's *Christabel* (1816). The name is still used in Ireland today.

Gerard [*Gearárd*] (m) Germanic, 'spear hard'. The

Normans introduced the name to Ireland, where a certain confusion with *Gerald* arose. It is still quite popular in Ireland today, owing to the influence of St Gerard Majella (died 1755).

Gertrude (f) Germanic, 'spear strength'. A name used in Ireland to anglicise *Grania*.

Gilbert [*Gilibeirt*] (m) Germanic, 'pledge bright'. A name introduced into Ireland by the Normans. It was used in Scotland to anglicise the Gaelic *Gilbride*.

Gilduffe [*Giolla Dubh*] (m) 'black servant'. A name which appears to have been once common in Derry.

Giles [*Éigid*] (m, f) Latin, 'kidlike'. As in England and Scotland, Giles has been used as both a masculine and feminine name. The Irish form, which is taken from an early source, presumably comes from Latin *Aegidius*. At the turn of the century the name was still used for both boys and girls in Co. Donegal, but it is now exclusively a masculine name.

Gill [*Giolla*] (m) An anglicised form of *Giolla* (q.v.) which occurs in the *Joyce* family, e.g. Gill Dubh Joyce (died 1774).

Gillespie (m) 'servant of the bishop'. A Gaelic name sometimes anglicised as *Archibald*. The Irish is *Giolla Easpaig;* the Scottish Gaelic is *Giolleasbuig*.

Gillian (f) A feminine form of *Julian*, name of uncertain meaning. It is used in Ireland in modern times.

Giolla (m) 'servant'. Irish Gaelic *giolla* corresponds to Scottish Gaelic *gille*. Gil was commonly prefixed to names, e.g. *Gilduffe, Gillespie*.

Giolla-na-naomh (m) 'servant of the saints'. This name was anglicised as *Nehemiah*.

Glasny [*Glaisne*] (m) A name formerly used in Ulster.

Gloria (f) Latin, 'glory'. This name was invented by the Irish playwright George Bernard Shaw and used in *You Never Can Tell* (1898). The actress Gloria Swanson, born in the same year, was probably chiefly responsible for spreading the name. Lareina Rule cites *Glori, Gloriana* and *Glory* as variants, but the form Gloriana may derive from Spenser's use of this name in *The Faerie Queene* (1590/6) for a character representing Elizabeth I.

Glorvina (f) This name appears to have been invented by the Irish writer, Lady Morgan, to name the daughter of an Irish prince in her novel *The Wild Irish Girl* (1806). It has occasionally been used as a first name.

Gobinet [*Gobnait*] (f) Derivative of *gob* 'mouth', 'beak', 'bill'. St Gobinet, a saint associated with Ballyvourney, was said to have been born in Clare. The name was anglicised as *Abigail*, with which it was at times used interchangeably. *Gobnat, Gobnet* and *Gubnet* are variants.

Gobnat (f) Variant of *Gobinet*.

Gobnet (f) Variant of *Gobinet*.

Godfrey [*Gofraidh*] (m) Germanic, 'god peace'. A name

which was translated into Irish as *Gofraidh, Gothfraidh* and *Gothraidh. Gorry* is a variant.

Gordon [*Gordan*] (m) A Scottish surname, thought to be derived from a placename in Berwickshire, which came into use as a first name, first in Scotland then throughout Britain. It became popular in the nineteenth century, chiefly in honour of General Gordon (1833-85).

Gordon was introduced into Ireland from Scotland. The first recorded Irish bearer was a son of Sir Phelim O'Neill, called after the family name of his Scottish grandfather, the Marquess of Huntly.

Gorry (m) Variant of *Godfrey.*

Grace (f) A name used in Ireland to anglicise *Grania.*

Graeme (m) An alternative spelling of *Graham,* recorded in Northern Ireland.

Graham [*Gréachán*] (m) Also *Graeme.* Anglo-Saxon, 'grey home'. The surname of a Scottish family which is now used as a first name. It occurs occasionally in Ireland.

Grania [*Gráinne*] (f) 'grain goddess'. In Irish legend Grania, Finn Mac Cool's betrothed, eloped with Dermot, his follower. Grania Mhaol Ni Mhaolmhaigh, in English, Grace O'Malley was queen of the Western Isles of Ireland in the sixteenth century. The name has been anglicised as *Grace* and *Gertrude.*

Granna (f) Evidently a form of *Grania,* borne by a daughter of Sir Edward O'Brien, Bt., of Dromoland, who died in 1837.

Gregory [*Greagóir*] (m) Greek, 'watchful one'. The Irish form of the name corresponds to Early English *Gregour,* Scottish *Gregor,* French *Gregoire* and German *Gregor.*

Gruagach (m) An Irish word, deriving ultimately from *gruaig,* 'hair', and meaning literally 'hairy one'. It normally signified 'magician' or 'giant'; but in Omeath, where it was used as a first name, it signified 'hero'.

Gubnet (f) Variant of *Gobinet.*

H

Hamlet (m) This name has been thought to be a form of Germanic *Hamo, Hamon,* 'home', but an alternative etymology has been put forward. The Norsemen, when they came to Ireland, brought with them the name *Olaf,* which was gaelicised as *Amhlaoibh.* It has been suggested that a modified form of this was re-exported to Scandinavia and in due course became Hamlet. Shakespeare has made the name well known, and he gave the variant name, *Hamnet,* to his son.

Hannah (f) A form of *Anne* which was once common in Ireland. It was also used as a pet form of *Johanna* and *Nora.*

Harold [*Aralt*] (m) Germanic, 'army power'. This was introduced into Ireland by the Norsemen, who used the spelling *Harald.* The name was given to Harold's Cross in

Dublin.

Hazel (f) A tree name which appears to have been invented in the nineteenth century. It is used from time to time in Ireland.

Heather (f) A plant name which seems to have originated in the nineteenth century, when botanical names became fashionable.

Heber [*Éibhear*] (m) There is a Hebrew name *Heber,* meaning perhaps 'companion', but the Irish Heber is completely unrelated. It may have originated in Cape Clear Island, and it is a phonetic translation into English of the Irish name *Éibhear,* the name of the son of the legendary leader Milesius. Heber was particularly popular in Ulster, and sometimes it was anglicised as *Ivor.*

Hector [*Eachtar*] (m) A Greek name of doubtful meaning which was used to anglicise *Eachann* in Scotland. It occurs occasionally in Ireland.

Helen [*Léan*] (f) Greek, 'bright one'. A name made famous by the legendary Greek beauty. It became popular throughout the Christian world due to St Helena (*c.* 248-327), mother of Constantine the Great. It is quite frequently bestowed in Ireland, and it is the source of a number of names, e.g. *Elaine* and *Eleanor. Nellie,* a pet form, is sometimes used as an independent name.

Helena [*Léana*] (f) The Latin form of *Helen,* used from time to time in Ireland.

Henrietta/Henriette (f) Feminine forms of *Henry,* used occasionally in Ireland in the early part of this century.

Henry [*Anraí*] (m) Germanic, 'home ruler'. A name introduced by the English. It became popular amongst the native population, the Gaelic forms becoming *Anrai, Annraoi, Einri, Hanraoi.* Henry Joy MacCracken was an eighteenth-century Ulster rebel. Today the name is no longer greatly used.

Herbert [*Hoireabard*] (m) Germanic, 'army bright'. This is a rare name in Ireland, but it enjoyed a certain vogue around the turn of the century.

Heremon [*Eireamhón*] (m) In Irish legend, Heremon was the son of Milesius. The name was used on Cape Clear Island, and it was sometimes anglicised as *Irving* or *Irwin.*

Hermon (m) Variant of *Heremon.*

Hewney [*Uaithne*] (m) An early name, sometimes anglicised as *Anthony. Oney, Owney and Oyney* are variant forms.

Hierlath (m) Variant of *Jarlath.*

Hiero (m) Greek, 'holy'. St Hiero (died 885) was an Irish martyr.

Hilary [*Hioláir*] (m, f) Latin, 'joyful'. A name occasionally used in Ireland. The Irish form may have been influenced by French *Hilaire.*

Hilda [*Hilde*] (f) Anglo-Saxon, probably 'war'. This is not a common name in Ireland.

Hisolda (f) Variant of *Iseult.*

Hodierna (f) A name which is perhaps taken from the Latin liturgy and used for children born about the time of the Epiphany. It has been used in Ireland, e.g. Hodierna de Gernon was granddaughter of the last king of Connacht.

Honor (f) Latin, 'honour'. A name brought to Ireland by the Normans. It became popular, giving rise to the native form *Nora(h). Ohnicio* and *Onora* are variants.

Honora (f) Variant of *Honor.*

Honoria (f) Perhaps a variant of *Honor. Hanoria* may be a further variant.

Hubert [*Hoibeard*] (m) Germanic, 'mind bright'. An uncommon name in Ireland. The Gaelic form was sometimes translated *Hugh.*

Hugh [*Aodh*] (m) Germanic, perhaps 'heart'. In both Ireland and Scotland Hugh was used to translate *Aodh.* In Ireland it was also used to translate *Hoibeard,* the Gaelic for *Hubert.* It is now quite widespread.

Humphrey [*Unfrai*] (m) A Germanic folk name *Huni,* 'peace'. Unfrai is the true Irish form, but Humphrey has been used as a translation of *Amhlaoibh,* the Irish form of *Olaf.* Humphrey O'Sullivan (*c.* 1780-1837) was an Irish language diarist. It is not a common name today.

Hyacinth (m) Greek, 'purple'. A name formerly used in Ireland, presumably to translate a native name.

I

Ian [*Ion*] (m) This name represents *Iain,* the Scottish Gaelic form of *John,* cognate with Irish Gaelic *Eoin.* It is ocasionally used in Ireland. The Irish language form, *Ion,* is taken from the diary of Humphrey O'Sullivan (*c.* 1780-1837).

Ibernia (f) Variant of *Hibernia.*

Ida (f) Variant of *Ita.* There is also a Germanic name *Ida,* used in England in the Middle Ages and revived there in the nineteenth century – a revival which may have influenced the increase in use of the Irish *Ida.*

Ierne (f) The Greek name for Ireland. It has been recorded as a given name.

Ignatius [*Éigneachán*] (m) The name Ignatius, sometimes explained as meaning 'fiery one', is in fact of unknown derivation. The Spanish form, *Inigo,* became the form used in Britain, while the Latin *Ignatius* became popular in Ireland, no doubt due to St Ignatius Loyola (1548-98), founder of the Jesuits. It was equated with the native name *Éigneachán* or *Igneachán* which, according to O'Hart, means 'force person'. St Ignatius' College is a well-known Jesuit school in Galway.

Ina [*Aghna*] (f) Perhaps an Irish form of *Agnes.*

Ion (m) This name may be Greek *Ion,* 'moon man'. It has been explained as a variant of *Ian,* but this seems unlikely;

and it is even less likely to be *Ion,* the Basque form of *John.* It was used in the *Trant* family in the nineteenth century.

Irene (f) Greek, 'peace'. A name which was used by the Byzantines and imported into England in the late nineteenth century. It presumably spread from there to Ireland. It is sometimes pronounced with two syllables; sometimes with three, as in the original Greek.

Irial (m) An early name which, Woulfe informs us, was used chiefly by the *O'Farrells, O'Kennedys* and *O'Loughlans.*

Irving (m) Anglo-Saxon, 'sea friend'. A name used to anglicise *Heremon.*

Irwin (m) Variant of *Irving,* also used to anglicise *Heremon.*

Isaac [*Iosóg*] (m) Hebrew, 'he may laugh'. A rare name in Ireland. *The Annals of the Four Masters* note the death of an Isaac O Maolfoghmair in 1235. The name was used in the *Glenny* family of Co. Down. *Iosac* and *Iosoc* are Irish language variants.

Isabel [*Isibéal*] (f) The French seem to have bestowed the translation *Isabelle* on Elizabeth of Hainault, wife of Philip Augustus (1165-1223). King John (1167-1216) married Isabelle of Angouleme, and she brought the name to England. The forms Isabel and *Isabella* took root there, and spread to Ireland, becoming the first versions of *Elizabeth* to be used there. See also *Sybil.*

Isabella (f) A variant of *Isabel* which was very popular in Ireland at the turn of the century, but is much less so now.

Iseult (f) According to Arthurian legend, Iseult, the lover of Tristram (or Tristan), was an Irish princess. The name is perhaps Germanic, 'ice rule'; perhaps Welsh, 'beautiful to see'. Yonge regards it as essentially the same name as *Adsaluta,* the name of a Celtic goddess. Iseult occurs in Ireland in modern times, no doubt because of its Irish associations. *Isolda, Hisolda, Yseult, Ysolte* and *Izett* are variants.

Isleen (f) Variant of *Ashling.*

Ismenia (f) This name may be of Irish origin, and it was certainly used in Ireland up to 1800. *Ismena* is a variant.

Ismey (f) A name of doubtful origin. It is possibly Irish and it was used in Ireland in the eighteenth century. *Ismay* is a variant.

Isolda (f) Variant of *Iseult.*

Ita [*Ide*] (f) 'thirst'. St Ita was associated with Killeedy in Co. Limerick, and her name is used in Ireland today. *Ida* is a variant.

Ivan (m) The Russian, Ukrainian and Bulgarian form of *John,* sometimes used in western countries. It has been recorded in Ireland.

Ivo (m) Germanic, 'yew'. A name, cognate with French *Yves,* which has been used in Ireland in the *de Vesci* family.

Ivor [*Íomhar*] (m) This name probably comes from Norse

Ivarr, the name of a number of kings of Dublin. However, there was an Irish saint called *Ibhar* who antedated the Norsemen. Ivor was also used to anglicise *Éibhear* (see *Heber*).

Izett (f) A form of *Iseult*, perhaps peculiar to Ireland. It was recorded in 1891.

J

Jacinta (f) From Greek, 'purple'. This is the Spanish form of a Greek name. It is sometimes found in Ireland.

James [*Séamus*] (m) This name is widely used in Ireland, though recently its use has declined considerably. It is found in both its Irish and English forms, and in its pet form, *Jamie*. Ultimately it is a form of *Jacob*, in Hebrew *Aqob*, of uncertain meaning. In medieval Latin it became *Jacomus*, in Spanish *Jaime*, and in English *James*. For further information on its use in Ireland, see *Seamus*. *Iamus* is an Irish form used in the *Annals of Connacht*.

Jamie (m) Originally a pet form of *James*, chiefly associated with Scotland. On a number of occasions recently it has been given as an independent name in Ireland.

Jana (f) This unusual name is a feminine form of *John*. It was employed in the *Lowther* family of Co. Meath. *Jan*, another feminine form of John, has been noted in Northern Ireland.

Jane [*Sinéad*] (f) A well-known feminine form of *John*, coming ultimately from Old French *Jehane*, and gaelicised as *Sinéad*. Its popularity has declined greatly since 1900, but it is still quite widely used.

Janet [*Sinéidín*] (f) A diminutive of *Jane*.

Janice (f) A form of *Jane* sometimes used in Ireland.

Jarlath [*Iarfhlaith*] (m) 'tributary lord'. St Jarlath (died 550) established the bishopric of Tuam. *Hierlath* is a variant.

Jarmy (m) A form of *Dermot* employed by the *O'Kanes* and the *O'Mullans*. This name is a half-way point between *Dermot* and its anglicisation, *Jeremiah*.

Jason [*Iasan*] (m) Greek, 'healer'. The name of the leader of the Argonauts. It is rapidly becoming a fashionable name in Ireland, and is now widespread.

Jasper [*Geaspar*] (m) A name of unknown meaning. According to tradition it was the name of one of the Magi. It has been used in Ireland, but it is now rare. *Gasper* is a variant.

Jean [*Síne*] (f) A Scottish feminine form of *John* which is used from time to time in Ireland. See also *Sheena*.

Jeffrey (m) Variant of *Geoffrey*.

Jennifer (f) It means 'white wave'. The Cornish form of *Guinevere*, the name of the wife of King Arthur. It is frequently bestowed in Ireland today.

Jeremiah [*Irimias*] (m) Hebrew, 'may God exalt'. The name of an Old Testament prophet, used in Ireland to anglicise

Dermot. It was once frequently used but it is now much rarer.

Jeremy (m) The English form of *Jeremiah* which has sometimes been used in Ireland.

Jerome (m) Greek, 'holy name'. St Jerome (*c.* 347-419) translated the Bible into the Latin version known as the Vulgate. The true Irish forms are *Cirine* and *Iarom*, but Jerome has generally been used in Ireland as an anglicisation of *Dermot*.

Joan [*Siobhán*] (f) A feminine form of *John*, coming from Latin *Jo(h)anna*. It was brought to Ireland by the Anglo-Normans and was gaelicised as *Siobhán*, of which *Siún* is a somewhat slurred variant.

Joanna (f) A form of *Joan*, once fairly popular, but it has now given way to *Joanne*.

Joanne (f) A recent feminine version of *John*, formed from *Joan* or *Joanna*. It is now thoroughly established in Ireland.

Johanna (f) A feminine form of *John*, once popular but now obsolescent. *Hannah* was a pet form.

John [*Seán*] (m) Hebrew, 'God has favoured'. An enormous number of Irishmen have borne either this name or one of its Irish forms: *Eoin*, *Sean*, *Seon*, *Shaun*, *Shawn* or *Shane*. Feminine forms of John include *Jane*, *Jean*, *Joan*, *Johanna*, *Joanna*, *Shona* and *Jana*.

Jonah [*Íona*] (m) Hebrew, 'dove'. A name occasionally used in Ireland. Jonah Barrington was an eighteenth century Irish writer.

Jonathan [*Ionatán*] (m) Hebrew, 'God's gift'. The first name of the Irish writer, Jonathan Swift (1667-1745). Jonathan Chetwood was a member of the Irish Parliament in 1797. Jonathan is increasingly popular in Ireland today.

Joseph [*Seosamh*] (m) Hebrew, 'God added'. Woulfe notes that this name was only becoming really popular in Ireland in his day – his book, *Irish Names for Children*, appeared in 1923. Its use as a first name is due to St Joseph, husband of the Blessed Virgin. There was an Irish St Joseph, bishop of Tallaght. The usual Irish form is *Seosamh;* others are *Iosaf, Iosep, Ioseph, Seacas, Seosap* and *Seosaph*.

Josephine [*Seosaimhín*] (f) A name which derives from the Empress Josephine (1763-1814), wife of Napoleon, whose real name was *Josepha* (French *Josèphe*).

Joyce (f) A name occasionally used in Ireland. It is a feminine form of the Celtic masculine name *Jodoc*, once used in Brittany.

Judith (f) Hebrew, 'Jewess'. A name used to anglicise *Síle* (see *Sheila*) and *Siobhan*.

Julia [*Iúile*] (f) A Roman name, a feminine of *Julius*, which is of uncertain meaning. It was used to anglicise the Irish names, *Síle* (see *Sheila)* and *Siobhan*.

Julie (f) A pet form of Juliet, now sometimes used as an independent name, and becoming increasingly popular.

Juliet (f) A feminine form of *Julius*, popularised by Shakespeare's *Romeo and Juliet*.

Junan/Junanan (m) Variants of *Adamnan*.

Juno (f) A Latin name which may mean 'young', and the name of the queen of the Roman gods. It was used in Ireland to anglicise *Una*, but its true Irish forms are *Iunainn* and *Iúnó*. Sean O'Casey used the name in his play *Juno and the Paycock* (1924).

Justin (m) Latin, 'just'. In Ireland this name was equated with *Saerbhreathach*, 'noble judge'. It is frequently used in the *MacCarthy* family.

Juverna (f) A Latin name for Ireland, used occasionally as a first name.

K

Kane (m) Use of Kane as a first name presumably comes from the surname. *Kane* is a common surname in Ulster, translating the Gaelic *O Cathain*, while is the Isle of Man it translates *MacCathian*. It may sometimes derive from the feminine first name *Keina*, perhaps Welsh, signifying 'beautiful'. At other times, it may derive from the placename *Caen*, or from Anglo-Saxon *Cana*. *Kane* is becoming a popular first name in Australia.

Karen (f) A form of *Katherine*, ultimately of Danish origin. It is now well established in Ireland. The pleasant combination of *Karen-Ann* has been recorded in Northern Ireland.

Kate (f) A pet form of *Katherine* sometimes given as a separate name.

Katherine [*Catraoine*] (f) A Greek name of uncertain meaning, sometimes mistakenly connected with *katharos*, 'pure'. The name was brought to Western Europe in the Middle Ages by returning crusaders, and it became established in Ireland. *Kate* and *Katie* are pet forms which have both been used independently. Other forms include *Catherine, Kathleen, Karen,* and *Catriona*.

Kathleen [*Caitlín*] (f) A form of *Katherine* now closely identified with Ireland. The Spanish form of Katherine was *Catalina;* the Old French form was *Cateline;* and these were presumably related to the Middle English *Catlin*, whence the Irish *Kathleen, Cathleen*.

Kean (m) Variant of *Cian* (see *Cain*).

Keelan (m) Variant of *Killian*.

Keith (m) A Scottish placename, used first as a surname and then as a first name. It has recently become quite popular with Irish parents.

Kellach (m) Variant of *Ceallach*, 'strife' (now obsolete).

Kelly (f) An Irish surname which is now used as a feminine first name. Its meaning is uncertain. In the case of the surname *O'Kelly* it probably derived from *ceallach*, 'strife', but the O' Kellys were distinct from the *MacKellys* of East

Connacht.

There is also the possibility that it comes from Kelly in Devon, a placename meaning 'wood', or from a couple of Scottish placenames. There is, in addition, a Manx surname Kelly, of Gaelic origin.

Kennedy [*Cinnéide*] (m) Although Wolfe gives this name as meaning 'helmeted head', it in fact means 'ugly head'. It is better known as a surname than as a first name, but it was none the less used as a first name in Ireland in the Middle Ages. King Kennedy of Munster was the father of Brian Boru, as a result of which it came to be employed in the *O'Brien* family.

Kenneth [*Cionaod*] (m) This name is usually associated more with Scotland than Ireland, but it seems to have been quite popular in Ireland during the Middle Ages in the form of *Cinaed*. The Name *Coinneach* (English, *Canice)* was also translated into English as Kenneth. Kenneth Mac Alpine (died *c.* 860) was king of Scots, whose reign united the Picts with the decendants of the Irish settlers in Scotland. *Cinaeth* O Hartagain (died 975) was an Irish poet.

Kenny (m) Variant of *Canice.*

Kerill [*Coireall*] (m) An Irish name which has been anglicised as *Cyril.*

Kermit (m) Variant of *Dermot,* and the name of a frog in the American television series *The Muppet Show.*

Kerry (f) An Irish placename now used as a girls' first name. Amongst the Boston Irish it is regarded as a form of *Katherine.*

Kevan [*Caomhán*] (m) 'little handsome one'. A name that was on occasion 'disguised' by Latin *Pulcherius,* 'beautiful one'.

Kevin [*Caoimhín*] (m) 'comely birth'. St Kevin (died *c.* 618), a Leinsterman, founded the monastery of Glendalough. The name is becoming more and more popular in Ireland. It is also much used in Britain, the United States and Canada.

Kian (m) Variant of *Cian.*

Kieran [*Ciarán*] (m) 'little dark one'. St Kieran was an Irish bishop who, it is said, may have antedated St Patrick and been a hermit at Saighiar. St Kieran's birthplace was Cape Clear, a vicinity particularly associated with this first name. Another St Keiran founded the great monastery of Clonmacnoise. The name in both its English and Irish forms is popular today. *Kieron, Queran* and *Kyran* are variants.

Kieron (m) A spelling variant of *Kieran.*

Killian [*Cillian*] (m) A diminutive of *ceallach* 'strife'. St Killian was an early martyr at Wurzburg. The name is still in use in modern times. *Keelan* is a variant.

Kyran (m) Variant of *Kieran.*

Kyras (m) A curious name, perhaps peculiar to Ireland. It may be a form *Cyrus* (=Persian, 'enthroned'). Kyras Tully (died 1637) was dean of Clonfert.

L

Laetitia (f) A variant spelling of *Letitia*.

Laoghaire (m) 'calf-herder'. Laoghaire, king of Tara, was said to have had a confrontation with St Patrick. The name is pronounced something like *Leary*. Dun Laoghaire ('Laoghaire's Fort') is the name of an important town in Ireland, south of Dublin.

Laughlin (m) A spelling variant of *Loughlin*.

Laura (f) Latin, 'laurel'. A name sometimes used in Ireland.

Laurence [*Labhrás*] (m) Latin, 'of Laurentum'. This name was used to translate the name of St *Lorcan* (Laurence) O'Toole (died 1180). Lawrence was introduced into Ireland by the Anglo-Normans and became in Irish *Labhrás*.

Leila [*Lil*] (f) A saint's name of obscure meaning. It is possibly connected with the Laelian gens of Rome, but this seems unlikely. It is a very old name which continues in use today.

Leo [*Leon*] (m) Latin, 'lion'. This name was adopted in Ireland when Gioacchino Vincenzo Pecci (1810-1903) became Pope Leo XIII in 1873. It was readily translated into Irish as *Leon*, the Irish word for a lion, and it is now firmly established.

Letitia (f) Latin, 'joy'. *Laetitia* is also found. In Ireland it is translated as *Eilis*, which is in fact Irish for *Elizabeth*. A variant *Lettice* was recorded in Ireland in 1711.

Lewis (m) The English form of *Louis*, sometimes used in Ireland to anglicise the native names of *Laoiseach* (see *Lysagh*) and *Lughaidh*.

Lewy (m) A phonetic English rendering of the Irish name *Lughaidh*.

Liam (m) The Irish form of *William*, now widespread. It is, of course, the second syllable of William, which was once translated as *Uilliam*, a name also used for the fox, corresponding to *Reynard* in English. The form *Bhullaidh* (pronounced *Wully*) was sometimes used for King William III (1650-1792). Liam was originally a pet form, but it is now established as the Irish translation. *Liam na Lasoige* is an Irish name for the Will o' the Wisp or *ignis fatuus*.

Lily [*Lile*] (f) A plant name coming from the Latin name for the flower.

Linda (f) A name derived from German *Lind*, 'serpent', 'snake', which is now becoming quite popular in Ireland. It is supposed – wrongly – to be connected with Spanish *linda*, 'pretty'. The variant *Lynda* is also found. An early Irish masculine name, *Nathair*, has exactly the same meaning. By tradition the serpent signifies wisdom.

Lisa (f) Originally a pet form of *Elizabeth*, but now an independent name. It is increasingly popular in Ireland today.

Lloyd (m) Welsh, 'grey'. A name sometimes found in Ireland.

Lorcan [*Lorcán*] (m) 'little fierce one'. St Lorcan O'Toole (died 1180) was one of Ireland's most famous saints. He was abbot of Glendalough and later, at the time of the Norman Invasion of Ireland (1169), he was archbishop of Dublin.

Lorna (f) A name invented by R. D. Blackmore for his novel *Lorna Doone* (1869). It is sometimes found in Ireland.

Lorraine (f) A French placename which is quite popular as a first name in Ireland. Lorraine was the birthplace of St Joan of Arc, and the name is associated with her. It was originally known as the Kingdom of Lotharingia, deriving from *Lothair,* son of King Clovis of the Franks, whose name meant 'hear people'. He ruled from 855.

Loughlin [*Lochlainn*] (m) Lochlainn was originally the name of a land in Irish legend, then it was applied to the homeland of the Norsemen. The first name Loughlin may spring originally from *MacLochlainn,* 'son of the Scandinavian'. It became widespread in Ireland. *Lochlann* was a variant in Irish. *Laughlin,* a variant in English, was also used to translate *Leachlainn,* a short form of *Maeleachlainn* (see *Melaghlin, Malachy*). There is a similar Scottish name, *Lachlan,* probably 'heroic', 'warriorlike', from Gaelic *laoch.*

Louis (m) Germanic, 'hear fight'. French *Louis* was translated as *Lewis* in England, but Louis itself was used in Ireland to translate the native names *Lughaidh* and *Lysagh.* It comes from the same root as *Clovis,* the name of a Frankish king. Other variants are *Lodowick, Ludovic,* and *Lutwidge.* In Wales the name was used to anglicise *Llewelyn* (*Lamhailín* in Irish), a name of uncertain meaning.

Louisa (f) A variant of *Louise,* popular at the turn of the century. It has now given way to Louise.

Louise [*Labhaoise*] (f) The feminine form of *Louis* which probably spread to Ireland from England where it was first noted in 1646. The Irish *Labhaoise* indicates that *Louisa* was the earliest form to occur in Ireland – Louisa was the usual form of the name in eighteenth-century England, and it was probably introduced to Ireland at about this time.

Lúcán (m) A derivative of Latin *Lucius* was *Lucianus,* which, as a cognomen, became *Lucanus.* This cognomen was borne by the poet Lucan, author of *De Bello Civilis,* popularly called the *Pharsalia,* and known to Irish readers as *In Cath Catharda.* His name is presumably the origin of the Irish *Lúcán.*

Lucius (m) This name probably comes from Latin *lux,* 'light'. It is firmly established in Ireland, where it is used to anglicise *Lachtna* and *Laoiseach* (see *Lysagh*). The Hibernian Sir Lucius O'Trigger appears in Sheridan's *The Rivals* (1775).

Lucy (f) A feminine form of *Lucius,* and the name of a third-century Sicilian virgin and martyr. In Ireland the name was equated with *Luighseach,* the feminine form of *Lughaidh.* The Italian form *Lucia* has also been noted in Ireland.

Lugh (m) Lugh Lamhfhada ('of the Long Arm') was the name of an early Irish hero of the Tuatha De Danaan who slew Balor of the Evil Eye. It is thought that he may originally have been a deity, perhaps imported from overseas – in the legend he travels to Ireland by boat. Lugh may in fact be identical with the continental Celtic god *Lugos* who gave his name to *Lughdunum* (modern Lyons).

Lughaidh (m) An early name for which the *O'Clery* family seem to have had an especial liking. It was anglicised as *Louis,* with which it coincides in pronunciation, and also as *Aloysius* and *Lewis,* the Provencal and English forms of that name.

Luke [*Lúcás*] (m) Greek, 'of Lucania'. A name which owes its popularity to St Luke. In England the name was established by the twelfth century, and it was probably brought from there to Ireland by the Anglo-Normans.

Lysagh [*Laoiseach*] (m) 'of Laois'. Laois is a county of Central Ireland – sometimes known by its English name, Leix – which was formerly called Queen's County. The change of name came after Independence. *Lysagh/ Laoiseach* was anglicised as *Lewis* or *Louis.*

M

Mabbina (f) This curious Irish name is perhaps an elaborate form of *Mabel.* It was used to anglicise *Maeve.*

Mabel [*Maible*] (f) An English form of the Latin name *Amabel,* which probably means 'lovable'. It has been used to anglicise *Maeve.*

Macanisius (m) 'son of Nis'. St Patrick was said to have consecrated St Macanisius (died 514), an early bishop.

Macartan (m) 'son of Cartan'. According to legend St Macartan was made bishop of Clogher by St Patrick.

Macha (f) 'plain'. The name of a legendary queen of Ireland.

Macmahon [*MacMathúna*] (m) An Irish surname used as a first name. The everyday word 'mayonnaise' ultimately derives from this name.

Madeline [*Madailein*] (f) The form of *Magdalen,* 'of Magdala', chiefly used in Ireland. Its English equivalent is *Madeleine.* The name is taken from St Mary Magdalen in the New Testament.

Madog (m) A Welsh form of the Irish name *Mogue,* occasionally found in Ireland.

Maelisa [*Maolíosa*] (m) 'servant of Jesus'. This name is cognate with the Scottish *Malise. Jesus – Latin,* 'God is salvation' (Hebrew *Jehoshua,* Aramaic *Yishu,* Greek *Iesous*) – is not itself used in Ireland, though it is found in

some countries. The Irish form is *Íosa*. Jesus is a form of
Joshua (Irish *Iósua*), a name which has been occasionally
used in Ireland. In Hellenistic times Jews names *Joshua*
equated the name with *Jason*.

Maeve [*Meadhbh*] (f) Perhaps, 'intoxicating one'. The name
of the legendary queen of Connacht, who led an invasion
of Ulster and was held at bay by Cuchulain until help
arrived. Maeve may originally have been a goddess.
Attempts to identify her with the English fairy queen Mab
have not proved successful. Connacht was termed *Crioch
Mheadhbha* ('Maeve's territory') and *Cuige Meadhbha*
('Maeve's province'). *Meave* is a spelling variant. *Mabbina,
Mabel, Margery* and *Maude* have been used as
anglicisations, but Maeve is used in its own right in modern
times. Maeve Binchy, the *Irish Times* columnist, is a modern
example.

Maggie (f) A pet form of *Margaret*. It was occasionally used
an as independent name in Ireland in the early part of the
twentieth century.

Mago (m) A name used in the Kilrush and Dingle areas. It
is now probably obsolete, but it appears to have been a
form of *Manus*.

Maguire [*MacUidhir*] (m) A surname of a prominent sept
of *Fermanagh* which was used as a first name. *Mac* signifies
'son' and *uidhir* is the genitive of *odhar*, 'dun-coloured'.

Mahon [*Mathghamhain*] (m) 'bear'. Mahon was a medieval
king of Munster (died 978), the brother of Brian Boru. The
name was often anglicised as *Matthew*. It corresponds to a
number of names in other languages: Latin *Ursus*,
American-Indian *Hatiya*. Scandinavian *Bjorn* and German
Berno.

Maille (f) Perhaps this is a native Irish name. It has been
translated as *Molly*.

Mailsi (f) Perhaps a native name. It has been translated as
Margery and *Molly*.

Mairona (f) A diminutive of *Máire*, the Irish for *Mary*.

Maiti (f) Nothing at all is known about this peculiar Irish
name, which is pronounced in English as *Matty*. One might
tentatively suggest that it is a feminine form of *Matthew*, or
a form of *Matilda*.

Majella (f) This name, sometimes found as a first name in
modern Ireland, is presumably the surname of St Gerard
Majella.

Malachy (m) Hebrew, 'my messenger'. This is the Irish form
of the name *Malachi* or *Malachias*. Malachy was used to
anglicise *Melaghlin*, the name of two high kings of Ireland,
and *Maolmaodhog*, the name of St Malachy (1095-1148),
bishop of Armagh. It is still used in Ireland today.

Malcolm [*Maolcholm*] (m) 'servant of St Columba'. This
Gaelic name is far more Scottish than Irish, even though it
commemorates one of the most celebrated Irish saints.

Yonge notes that strange latinisation *Milcolumbus*. Its widespread use in England is modern, but it has been known there from early times: a *Malcolum* is mentioned in the Domesday Book (1086).

Malone (m) An Irish surname meaning 'servant of St John', which at times may have become confused with Muldoon, 'servant of the fort'. Edward Malone (1741-1812) was a famous Irish Shakespearean scholar. Loughead notes its use as a first name.

Malvina (f) Perhaps a derivation of Gaelic *maol*, 'servant' or 'handmaid'. The name is an invention of James Macpherson. In his Ossianic poems (1765) Malvina is the lover of Oscar, grandson of Finn MacCool (see *Finn*). It has been used as a Christian name.

Manasses (m) Hebrew, 'one who makes forget'. In Derry an unsuccessful attempt was made to use this name to translate *Manus*.

Mane (m) Apparently a form of *Manus*.

Mannix (m) A name used in Ireland to anglicise *Munchin*.

Manus [*Mánús*] (m) Latin, 'great'. Charlemagne (742-814) was known in Latin as *Carolus Magnus*, and Magnus was adopted as a name by the Scandinavians who introduced it to Ireland. In Irish the *g* was eventually left unpronounced. It was particularly popular in Donegal and is still in use to this day. Magnus has been recorded in Northern Ireland. An attempt to anglicise Manus as *Manasses* in the Derry region failed. *Moses* was sometimes used to anglicise it. *Mane* is possibly a variant.

Maolmadhog [*Maolmaodhog*] (m) 'servant of St Mogue'. The Irish name of St *Malachy*.

Marcella [*Mairsile*] (f) A feminine diminutive of *Mark*, probably introduced into Ireland from France.

Margaret [*Mairéad*] (f) Greek 'pearl'. A name introduced into Scotland and England by St Margaret (*c.* 1046-93), queen of Scots, who was born in Hungary, where the name was familiar. The Anglo-Normans introduced it to Ireland and it became very popular. It is now declining sharply. The pet forms are *Peg* and *Peggy* (Irish *Peig* and *Peigi*) and *Maggie*. *Margot* and *Rita* are variants sometimes encountered in Ireland.

Margery (f) From *Margerie*, a French form of *Margaret*. Margery has been used in England since the thirteenth century. It has also been used in Ireland, sometimes to anglicise *Maeve* and *Mailsi*.

Maria [*Máiría*] (f) The Latin form of *Mary*, sometimes used in Ireland.

Marie (f) The French form of *Mary* which is used today in Ireland.

Marion [*Muireann*] (f) A diminutive of *Mary*. In Ireland it was used to anglicise *Muireann*, 'long-haired' (see *Morrin*).

Mark [*Marcas*] (m) Perhaps a derivative of *Mars*, the name of the Roman god of war, rendered in Irish as *Mars* and *Mart*. Its meaning is uncertain: Greek *marakos,* 'tender'; Latin *mas,* 'male'; and Celtic *marc,* 'horse' have also been suggested as possible origins. The name is international. It was introduced to Ireland by the Anglo-Normans, but it did not become a favourite until modern times. *Marcella* is a feminine diminutive

Marmaduke (m) This name, used also in the north of England, may be of Irish origin. The Domesday Book (1085-6) mentions the name *Melmidoc,* which is possibly an early form, and this readily translates into Irish as *Maelmaedoc,* 'servant of *Maedoc (=? Mogue).*

Martha [*Márta*] (f) This name is possibly a feminine of *mar,* the Aramaic work for 'lord'. It has been used to anglicise *More.*

Martin [*Máirtín*] (m) Probably a derivative of *Mars.* St Martin of Tours (*c.* 316-397) was reputed to be related to St Patrick, and the name became a popular one in Ireland. In England it tended to die out after the Reformation. The earlier Irish form was *Martán,* but Martin was imported by the Normans in the twelfth century.

Martina (f) A feminine form of *Martin,* popular amongst Irish parents of the mid-seventies.

Mary [*Máire*] (f) Probably the most widespread girls' name in Ireland, though at present its popularity is rapidly declining. It represents Hebrew, *Miriam;* Greek, *Mariam;* Latin, *Maria.* It is of uncertain derivation: the Hebrew root may be *rama,* 'long for'.

The name of the Blessed Virgin was little used in Ireland before the seventeenth century, probably due to reverence. Indeed, even today in the Irish language *Máire* is the usual form employed, *Muire* being reserved for the Blessed Virgin. *Miriam,* the name of the sister of Moses in the Old Testament, is occasionally found, as are the Latin and French forms: *Maria, Marie.* Diminutives include *Marion* and *Mairona. Molly, Mollie* and *Polly* are pet forms which have been used independently. *Moira* seems to be an attempt to anglicise *Máire. Mears* was an Irish form of the name used in Kerry, clearly derived from the English Mary. See also *Maura* and *Maurya.*

Mary is sometimes given as a boys' middle name in Ireland, a custom also found in Spain and Italy.

Matadin (m) Also *Matudan.* A derivative of the early Irish *matad* (modern Irish *mada*), 'dog'. The Norse name *Modan* may have been a variant of this.

Matilda [*Maitilde*] (f) Germanic, 'might strife'. The Normans introduced this name to England, and it spread from there to Ireland.

Matthew [*Matha*] (m) Hebrew, 'God's present'. The name of one of the Apostles. It was translated into Irish as *Matha* and *Maitiú* – the latter, perhaps influenced by French

Matheu, tended to become confused with *Matthias,* which has the same derivation. Matthew was used in Ireland to anglicise *Mahon.*

Matthias [*Maitias*] (m) A variant of *Matthew* which is sometimes found in Ireland.

Matudan (m) Variant of *Matadin.*

Maude [*Máda*] (f) A Norman form of *Matilda,* coming from Flemish *Mahault.* It was used in Ireland to anglicise *Maeve.*

Maughold (m) 'son of Caldus'. St Patrick is said to have converted St Maughold (died *c.* 488), who became a bishop on the Isle of Man.

Maura (f) A feminine form of Latin *Maurus,* 'Moor'. In Ireland it is regarded as a form of *Mary.*

Maureen [*Máirín*] (f) A diminutive of *Máire,* the Irish for *Mary.* Mary itself is losing ground, but Maureen is increasingly used. It may have been reinforced by *Moreen,* a name of quite different origin. Maureen is frequently used in the United States and England. Maureen Toal and Maureen O'Hara are two contemporary Irish actresses; Maureen Potter is a popular Dublin comedienne.

Maurice [*Muiris*] (m) Latin, 'Moor'. A name used in Ireland amongst the Anglo-Normans. It has assimilated the native Irish name *Muirgheas,* 'sea choice'. *Moss* and *Mossy* are pet forms.

Maurine (f) Perhaps a variant of *Maureen.*

Maurya (f) A phonetic rendering of *Máire* used by J. M. Synge in his play *Riders to the Sea* (1904).

Maziere (m) A name employed in the *Brady* family. The earliest traced bearer is Sir Maziere Brady, Bt. (1796-1871). The name seems confined to this Irish family.

Meave (f) Variant of *Maeve.*

M(a)el [*Maol*] (m) 'servant'. A name occasionally used in Ireland. It is often found as a prefix in longer names, e.g. *Maelisa.*

Melaghlin [*Maeleachlainn*] (m) 'servant of St Secundinus'. Melaghlin is the true English form of Maeleachlainn, but *Malachy* was commonly used to translate it, and at present it seems to have completely replaced it. *Miles* was occasionally used as a translation.

Melchior [*Meilseoir*] (m) A name of eastern origin, perhaps meaning 'king'. It was said to have been the name of one of the Magi. In Ireland it was found in the vicinity of Youghal, Co. Cork.

Melissa (f) Greek, 'bee'. A name sometimes found in Ireland.

Merna (f) Variant of *Myrna.*

Meyler (m) A name derived from Welsh *Meilir* which was used to translate *Maelmuire,* 'servant of St Mary'. It now seems to be obsolete.

Miach (m) The name of the son of the pagan Irish god, Diancecht. It is perhaps derived from Latin *medicus,* 'physician'.

Michael [*Micheál*] (m) Hebrew, 'who is like God?' The name given to one of the archangels. In Ireland it only came into use after the sixteenth century, but it then became so common that many people look on it as a particularly Irish name.

The Irish form, Micheál, was given the phonetic rendering of *Meehaul* by James Stephens in his novel *The Crock of Gold* (1912). *Mick* is a common pet form, which in slang has come to mean an Irishman, and in the British Army the Irish Guards are referred to as 'the Micks'. *Mickey,* another pet form, has found fame in Walt Disney's creation, Mickey Mouse. Disney had the name's Irish associations in mind when he gave it to his celebrated character. *Mike* is an international pet form. Less common is *Mikey,* a form used in T. H. White's hilarious Irish novel, *The Elephant and the Kangaroo* (1947). *Miche* is a rare pet form.

Michael Collins was an Irish rebel, killed in 1922. Micheál MacLiammoir (1899-1978) was a well-known Irish actor.

Michan (m) St Michan was a Dublin monk. His name was given to St Michan's Church in the city.

Michelle (f) A French feminine version of *Michael* which seems popular amongst modern Irish parents. *Michele* is an alternative spelling. *Michaela,* another feminine form of Michael, also occurs.

Miles (m) A name of unknown meaning. It was used in Ireland as the equivalent of *Melaghlin, Maelmuire* and *Maolmordha. Meidhligh* was a Derry form of Miles, recasting the name into Irish. *Myles* is a spelling variant.

Milesius [*Mile*] (m) The name of the legendary leader of the invasion of Ireland by the Celts or Milesians. He was called *Míle Easpáin,* which may represent Latin *Miles Hispaniae,* 'soldier of Spain'.

Milo (m) The Old German form of *Miles,* used in Ireland to anglicise the same names. Milo O'Shea is a contemporary Irish actor.

Miranda (f) Latin, 'admirable'. This name was invented by Shakespeare for his play *The Tempest.* It is occasionally used in Ireland.

Mogue [*Maodhóg*] (m) A pet form of *Aidan* given to St Aidan of Ferns (died 626). The name was adopted into Welsh as *Madog.* In Ireland it was anglicised as *Aidan* by Protestants, and *Moses* by Catholics.

Moina (f) Boyer lists this as an Irish name, meaning perhaps 'noble'. She gives *Moyna* as an alternative spelling.

Moira (f) This seems to be an anglicised spelling of *Máire.* The name has spread to England. It was used as the name of a character in the novel *The Way Women Love* (1877) by E. Owens Blackburn. *Moyra* is a variant.

Molan [*Maolanfaidh*] (m) 'servant of storm'. The name of St Molan of Lismore (died 697).

Molly [*Maili*] (f) Originally a pet form of *Mary*, but now sometimes used independently. Molly was used to translate the native names *Maille* and *Mailsi*.

Mona(t) [*Muadhnait*] (f) 'little noble one'. A name used in its own right and also as a pet form of *Monica*.

Monica [*Moncha*] (f) The meaning of this name is uncertain; it is perhaps Greek 'alone' or Latin 'counsellor'. St Monica was the mother of St Augustine of Hippo (335-430). *Mona* is a pet form.

More [*Mór*] (f) 'great'. Once a widespread Irish name. It has been anglicised as *Agnes, Mary* and *Martha*.

Moreen [*Móirín*] (f) A diminutive of *More* which perhaps became confused with *Maureen*.

Morgan (m) Welsh, perhaps 'sea-born'. In Ireland this name was used to anglicise the native names, *Murchadh* and its West Connacht variant, *Brochadh*.

Morna [*Muirne*] (f) 'affection', 'beloved'. This was the name of Morna Dunroon, heroine of Harriet Jay's novel *The Dark Colleen* (1876). It has been used as a first name. *Myrna* is a variant, popular in the United States.

Morolt (m) In Arthurian legend Morolt was the brother of Iseult, princess of Ireland. The name is perhaps a form of *Murrough*.

Morrin [*Múireann*] (f) 'long haired'. This early Irish name has been anglicised as *Marion,* or even *Madge,* a pet form of *Margaret. Muirinn* was an Irish language variant.

Mortimer (m) Originally a surname, Mortimer derives from Mortemer, a place name in Normandy. In Ireland it is used to anglicise *Murtagh* and *Murrough*.

Moses [*Maoise*] (m) A name, possibly of Egyptian origin, signifying 'child'. It was used in Ireland to anglicise *Mogue* and *Manus*. Amongst the Anglo-Irish, Moses was used in the *Hill* family.

Moyra (f) A spelling variant of *Moira*.

Mugain (f) A feminine form of *mogh*, 'slave'. This was the name of a queen or goddess in Irish mythology.

Mulroona [*Maolruanaidh*] (m) A name used by the *O'Carroll* family, princes of Ely O'Carroll.

Munchin [*Mainchin*] (m) 'little monk'. St Munchin is associated with Limerick. *Mannix* was used as an anglicisation of this name.

Muriel (f) In Ireland this is the English form of *Muirgheal*, 'sea bright'. Muriel can also be traced to medieval Brittany and Normandy. It is probably Celtic; Yonge suggests that it comes from Greek and means 'myrrh', but this seems unlikely.

Murphy (m) 'sea warrior'. A widespread Irish surname. It means 'grandson of *Muirchu*', which is a combination of *muir,* 'sea' and *cu,* 'hound' (figuratively 'warrior'). It has now come to be used as a first name.

Murrough [*Murchadh*] (m) 'sea warrior'. An early name,

once very widespread. *Mortimer* was used as an anglicisation. *Morolt* is perhaps a variant.

Murtagh [*Muircheartach*] (m) 'sea expert'. A royal name in Ireland, the name of three kings of Tara, and a prince known as Muircheartach of the Leather Cloaks. *Mortimer* was used to anglicise it.

Myles (m) An alternative spelling of *Miles*. Brian O'Nolan (1911-66) used the pen-name Myles na Gopaleen – a name originally created by Dion Boucicault (1822-90) – for a number of his works and for his *Irish Times* column.

Myrna (f) Another form of *Morna*. Though Irish in origin, this name seems to be more used in the United States. *Merna* is a variant.

N

Naal (m) The name of an early Irish saint. His name is also given as *Natalis,* a Latin word meaning 'birth'. Naal may be a form of this word.

Nancy [*Nainsí*] (f) A pet form of *Anne* which is now sometimes used as an independent name.

Natasha (f) A Russian form of *Natalie*, 'Christmas', occasionally found in Ireland.

Nehemiah (m) Hebrew, 'God's consolation'. In Ireland this name was used to anglicise *Giolla-na-Naomh*. *Nehemias* Donnellan was archbishop of Tuam.

Neil (m) A form of *Niall*. It is used more in Scotland, but it is increasing in Ireland. *Neal* is a variant.

Nelda (f) A feminine form of *Neil* or *Niall*.

Nellie (f) A pet form of *Helen* which has occasionally been used as an independent name in Ireland.

Nessa (f) Originally, this was a pet form of *Agnes*, but it is now used as an independent name in Ireland.

Nessan [*Neasan*] (m) A name which was perhaps originally connected with the word *neas,* 'stoat'.

Nevan [*Naomhan*] (m) 'little saint'. A rare name in modern Ireland.

Niadh (m) 'champion'. St Niadh was venerated in Meath, and his name was given as a Christian name.

Niall (m) A derivative of *néall,* 'cloud', and the name of one of the most famous kings of Tara, Niall of the Nine Hostages, the founder of the Ui Neill dynasty of Irish kings. The *O'Neills,* a branch of that family, descend from Niall Black-Knee, who fell fighting against the Scandinavians in 917. Although used today, the name is yielding ground to its Scottish form, *Neil.* In Irish Niall rhymes with 'real'; in English it rhymes with 'phial'.

Niamh (f) 'bright'. In Irish mythology, Niamh, princess of the Land of Promise, departed with Ossian, son of Finn MacCool, for the Otherworld. The name is rapidly increasing in popularity in Ireland today. *Niav* is an anglicised spelling.

Nicholas [*Nicolas*] (m) Greek, 'victory people'. This name has been popular in Ireland since the Middle Ages. It is still quite frequently used.

Nicola (f) A feminine form of *Nicholas*. The original feminine form was *Nicole* – Nicola is in fact the masculine form used in Italy, where it has replaced the more masculine-sounding *Niccolo*. Nicola is now the established feminine form in Ireland.

Nigel (m) The history of this name is complex. The Scandinavians bore the Irish name *Niall* to Iceland where it became *Njal,* a form which 'returned' to Scandinavia, and from there went to Normandy where it was latinised as *Nigellus.* Nigel dates from the fifteenth century, and it has become the everyday English form. It is occasionally used in Ireland, but it is most used in Scotland, where it also occurs as *Neil.*

Noel [*Nollaig*] (m) Noel is French for 'Christmas', and the Irish Nollaig translates it exactly. The name enjoyed great popularity in Ireland in mid-century, but it is now declining.

Noelle [*Nollaig*] (f) French, 'Christmas'. A feminine form of *Noel.*

Nora(h) [*Nora*] (f) A form of *Honora*, of Irish origin. Nora is the commoner spelling, but the name's popularity is declining today. *Honoria,* a name particularly popular in the nineteenth century, may have been an elaboration of Nora(h) rather than a name taken directly from Latin. Nora was used by Ibsen in his play *A Doll's House* (1879). *Nonie* and *Hannah* are pet forms.

Noreen [*Noirin*] (f) A diminutive of *Nora* which occurs from time to time as an independent name.

Norlene (f) An elaboration of *Nora.*

Nuala (f) A short form of *Fionnuala* which was popular round about the middle of the century, but it is now little used.

O

Odanodan (m) Variant of *Adamnan.*

Odran (m) Variant of *Oran.*

Ogh(i)e (m) Variant of *Eochaidh.*

Ohnicio (f) An Irish variant of *Honora.*

Oho (m) Variant of *Eochaidh.*

Olga (f) A Russian name, ultimately derived from Germanic, 'holy'. It is rare in Ireland.

Olive (f) Latin, 'olive'. This name was used in Ireland to anglicise *Elva.* See also *Olivia.*

Oliver [*Oilibhéar*] (m) Perhaps a form of *Olaf* (see *Auliffe);* or perhaps from Old French, 'olive tree', or Old German, 'elf army'. This name, which appeared in England in the Middle Ages, would have all but disappeared amongst the native Gaels owing to their loathing of Oliver Cromwell. It was saved by being the name of St Oliver Plunket, archbishop of Armagh, executed by the English in 1681. Oliver St John Gogarty (1878-1957) was an Irish writer. Oliver has increased in popularity in recent years.

Olivia (f) A form of *Olive* used by Shakespeare in *Twelfth Night*. It became an established name in England in the eighteenth century, and it probably spread from there to Ireland, where use of the name is currently increasing.

Ona (f) Variant of *Una*.

Onan (m) A form of *Adamnan* found in Derry.

Oney (m) A form of *Hewney*.

Onora (f) A form of *Honora* used in Ireland, where it was recorded as early as 1634.

Oona(gh) (f) Variant of *Una*.

Oran [*Odhrán*] (m) A diminutive of *odhar*, 'green' or 'dun'. *Odran* is a variant.

Orinthia (f) This name was invented by the Irish playwright, George Bernard Shaw, for use in *The Apple Cart* (1929). It has since passed into general usage.

Orla [*Orfhlaith*] (f) 'golden lady'. A name which is increasing in popularity. It may also be spelt *Orlagh*. *Aurnia* is a variant.

Orna(t) [*Odharnait*] (f) A diminutive of *odhar*, 'dun' or 'green'.

Oscar (m) The name of a hero of legend, the grandson of Finn MacCool. Some writers assume that this is the Germanic name *Oscar*, 'divine spear', introduced into Ireland by the Scandinavians, but this is unlikely. The Finn legends probably antedate the Vikings, and a likelier derivation is Irish *oscar*, 'champion warrior'. The word in Irish can also mean 'jewel'. The use of the name in the Swedish royal family comes from the Gaelic source. The House of Bernadotte adopted it at Napoleon's instance – the Emperor had a predilection for Macpherson's Ossianic poems (1765). The Irish writer, Oscar Wilde (1854-1900) was named after a Swedish king.

Ossian [*Oisín*] (m) 'fawn'. The name of the son of the legendary hero, Finn MacCool, whose mother was said to have spent part of her existence as a deer. Ossian was supposed to have lived for a time in the Land of Promise. The Scottish writer, Macpherson, described his adventures in his Ossianic poems (1765) where the deeds of the Fianna are set entirely in Scotland.

Ounan (m) Variant of *Adamnan*.

Owen (m) A name used in Ireland to anglicise *Eoghan*, to which it equates phonetically. In Wales it represents *Euguein*. Both names mean 'well born'.

Ownah (f) Variant of *Una*.

Owney (m) Variant of *Hewney*.

Oynie (m) Variant of *Hewney*.

P

Pamela (f) Greek, 'all honey'. A name invented by Sir Philip Sidney (1554-86). It was popularised by Samuel Richardson's novel *Pamela* (1740), and this resulted in its use as a first name.

Parlan (m) Variant of *Partholon.*

Partholon [*Parthalón*] (m) .The name of a legendary invader of early Ireland – the first, so tradition has it, to come there after the Flood. His followers are referred to as the Partholonians. *Bartholomew, Barclay* and *Berkley* have all been employed to anglicise Partholon. It is still in use today. *Parlan* is a variant.

Patricia [*Pádraigín*] (f) Latin, 'noble'. The feminine form of *Patrick,* and a name which appears to have been known in early times. According to legend St Patricia died in Naples *c.* 665. The name is commonly supposed to have been recreated in eighteenth-century Scotland, but the evidence for this is doubtful. However, it has greatly increased in popularity in modern times, perhaps due to its royal bearer, Princess Patricia of Connaught. The Irish have, of course, welcomed the female equivalent of the names of their patron; it has been gaelicised as *Pádraigín,* formerly used only as a diminutive of *Pádraig.* The pet forms are *Pat* and *Paddy* – the latter is rather rare.

Patrick [*Pádraig*] (m) Latin, 'noble'. The Latin adjective *patricius* signified membership of the patricians, the aristocracy of ancient Rome. Although a name of Latin derivation, Patrick is regarded as the national name of Ireland. St Patrick (*c.* 385-461), patron saint of Ireland, was an early missionary to the country. It has, in fact, been suggested that there may have been more than one early Christian preacher with this name.

At first the name was not used in Ireland, presumably out of reverence, but compounds such as *Gilpatrick* and *Maelpatrick* were found. In due course the Irish started using Patrick on its own. It was established by the seventeenth century, when Patrick Sarsfield was the Jacobite earl of Lucan.

At one time there was an attempt to amalgamate Patrick with *Peter.* While this did not meet with success, St Patrick's Day is now sometimes called *Peadar's (Peter's) Day.*

The usual Irish form of Patrick is *Pádraig.* Variants include *Padraic, Patric* and *Peyton. Pha(e)drig* was a rather unsatisfactory variant. *Pat, Paddy, Patsy* and *Pa* are pet forms in Ireland; *Pate* and *Patie* were used in Scotland. *Pádraigín,* an Irish diminutive, is now also used to translate *Patricia.* Patrick is often given in conjunction with *Joseph,* and bearers are sometimes called *Pa Joe.*

The surname *Fitzpatrick* is a Norman form of the Irish *Mac an Giolla Pádraig,* 'son of the servant of Patrick'.

Patrick Pearse, the rebel leader of 1916, no doubt added

to the name's popularity.

Paul [*Pól*] (m) Latin *paulus*, 'little'. The Roman name of *Saul* (Hebrew, 'asked for'; Irish, *Sol*), one of the foremost early Christians. Paul had its beginnings amongst the Aemilian gens, a tribe noted for their smallness. The name is used in Ireland, as in other Christian countries. It has become very popular in modern times.

Paula (f) A feminine of *Paul*, sometimes used in Ireland.

Pauline [*Póilín*] (f) A feminine form of *Paul* from its derivative, *Paulinus*.

Penelope (f) A Greek name of uncertain meaning, borne by the wife of Odysseus. In Ireland it was used to anglicise *Finola*. *Penny* and *Nappy* are short forms.

Perce (m) Presumably a variant of *Pierce*, itself a variant of *Peter*. It was borne by one of the *Butler* family, Lord Dunboyne, the third son of Edward Butler, who was referred to as both Perce and Peter.

Peregrine (m) Latin, 'wanderer', 'pilgrim'. This name has its origin in the seventh century in Italy where a hermit, said to have been an Irish prince, was known as *il pellegrin;* he was later canonised as St Peregrine, *Pellegrino* in Italian. Peregrine occurs in England from the thirteenth century onwards, and it was used in Ireland to anglicise *Cuchoigcriche*, 'hound of the border', a Westmeath and Offaly name (now obsolete).

Peter [*Peadar*] (m) According to the New Testament, *Cephas* (Aramaic, 'rock') was the name bestowed by Christ upon the Apostle Simon. This was translated into Greek as *Petros*, intended as a masculine form of *petra*, 'rock'. The Norman form *Piers/Pierce* was the usual one in Ireland until comparatively modern times, but nowadays Peter is popular. At one stage there was an unsuccessful attempt to amalgamate Peter with *Patrick*. The Irish form *Peadar* strongly resembles the Welsh *Pedr*.

Phadrig (m) Variant of *Patrick*, doubtless from *Phadraig*, the vocative of *Padraig*.

Phaedrig (m) Variant of *Patrick*. Sir Phaedrig Lucius Ambrose O'Brien, baron of Inchiquin and claimant to the Irish throne, is a contemporary example.

Phelan (m) A diminutive of *faol*, ('wolf'). This is more common as a surname, but it has been given as a first name.

Phelim(y) (m) Variant of *Felim(id)*.

Phiala (f) The name of a fifth-century Irish saint who was killed in Cornwall.

Philip [*Pilib*] (m) Greek, 'lover of horses'. The name of a number of kings of Macedonia, notably Philip II (382-336 B C), the father of Alexander the Great. It spread throughout the Near East in the Hellenic Era. St Philip was one of the Apostles. The name was established in Ireland by the Anglo-Normans and it is popular today. *Filib* and *Filip* are Irish language variants.

Philomena (f) Greek, 'loved'. The supposed relics of a saint of this name were discovered in 1802. The name became popular in Ireland, but, when the Vatican suppressed the cultus, a sharp drop in the number of Irish girls given this name occurred.

Phyllis (f) Greek, 'leafy'. An ancient name which became popular in England at about the turn of the century. It was doubtless exported from there to Ireland.

Pierce [*Piaras*] (m) The Norman French form of *Pierre* (the French for *Peter*) was *Piers*, and this was once the usual form in England, where Peter was unknown in the early Middle Ages. The English brought Piers/Pierce to Ireland and there the Gaelic forms *Piaras* and *Fiaras* sprang up, the latter giving rise to the surnames *Kerrisk, Kierse* and *MacKerrisk*. The name has been used in modern times. *Feories* was formerly a variant.

Piers (m) Variant of *Pierce*.

Polly [*Paili*] (f) A pet form of *Mary* (via *Molly*) which is now sometimes used as an independent name.

Q

Quentin (m) Variant of *Quintin*.

Queran (m) Variant of *Kieran*.

Quinn (m) An Irish surname meaning 'counsel', which is sometimes used as a Christian name.

Quintin (m) Latin, 'fifth'. This name was used in Ireland, together with its variants *Quentin* and *Quinton*, to anglicise *Cooey*.

Quinton (m) Variant of *Quintin*.

R

Rachel [*Ráichéal*] (f) Hebrew, 'ewe'. An Old Testament name which has become established in Ireland in modern times.

Ralph [*Rádhulbh*] (m) Germanic, 'counsel wolf'. The Irish form corresponds to Anglo-Saxon *Raedwulf*, Old Norse *Radulfr*. It was common amongst the medieval Anglo-Normans in Ireland. *Ralf* in Irish is a personal name used for the Cromwellian soldier.

Ranalt (f) A name dating from the twelfth century: Ranalt, daughter of Awley O'Farrell, king of Conmacne, married Hugh O'Connor, the last king of Connacht.

Randal(l) (m) Anglo-Saxon, 'shield wolf'. A name used to anglicise *Raghnall*, itself the Irish form of *Reginald*.

Randolph [*Rannulbh*] (m) In Ireland this name represents the Frankish *Randulf*, 'shield wolf', whereas in England it is a form of *Randal*.

Raymond [*Réamonn*] (m) Germanic, 'counsel protection'. A name brough to England by the Normans. It spread from there to Ireland, where it is a popular name today. See also *Redmond*.

Rebecca (f) Hebrew, perhaps 'heifer'. An Old Testament name which has occasionally been used in Ireland. *Rebekah,* an alternative spelling, has also been noted, though this is much rarer.

Redmond (m) An Irish form of *Raymond,* sometimes encountered in modern times. John Redmond, an Irish politician in the early part of the twentieth century, may have influenced usage. *Redmund,* presumably a spelling variant, has also been noted.

Regina (f) Latin, 'queen'. A name used in Ireland as the equivalent of the native name *Riona.*

Reginald [*Rá(gh)nall*] (m) Germanic, 'power might'. A name brought to Ireland by both the Scandinavians, who used the form *Rognvaldr,* and the Anglo-Normans, who employed the form *Ragenald. Reynold* was a Middle English form.

Renan (m) Variant of *Ronan.*

Renny [*Rathnait*] (f) 'little prosperous one'. A name which may now be obsolete. *Ranait* is an Irish language variant.

Revelin [*Roibhilín*] (m) A name of Ulster origin, found in the Co. Down area. It was sometimes anglicised as *Ro(w)land.*

Richard [*Risteard*] (m) Germanic, 'ruler hard'. A popular name in medieval England. It was introduced into Ireland and became established there. Richard Steele (1672-1729) was an Irish essayist, and Richard Brinsley Sheridan (1751-1816) was a famous Irish playwright. Richard Harris is a contemporary Irish actor and singer. It is a popular name in Ireland today.

Rickard [*Riocárd*] (m) An Irish variant of *Richard;* cf. Old German *Ricohard.* The name continues to be used on a small scale in Ireland.

Ringan (m) An Irish form of *Ninian,* the name of the saintly British missionary and bishop of Whithorn (died *c.* 432).

Riona [*Rioghnach*] (f) Perhaps 'queenly', derived from *rioghan,* 'queen'. *Regina* was used to translate this name.

Robert [*Roibeárd*] (m) Germanic, 'fame bright'. This name was *Robert* in French, *Ruprecht* (English *Rupert)* in German. It was frequently used in Ireland amongst the Anglo-Normans, and *Roibeard, Ribeart, Ribirt* and *Riobart* were Irish language forms. *Robin* (Irish *Roibin)* was originally a pet form, but it now sometimes occurs as an independent name. The popularity of Robert is increasing in Ireland today. Rupert also sometimes occurs. Robert Emmet (1778-1893) was an Irish patriot. Robert of Eire was the name of the Irish hero in the novel *Warlord of Ghandor* (1977) by Dell DowDell.

Robuck (m) This curious name has been used in the *Galway* family: it was borne by Robert *Kinvan* (died 1635), son of Robert Kinvan.

Roderick (m) Germanic, 'fame rule'. A name used in

Ireland to anglicise *Rory*.

Rodney (m) Anglo-Saxon, 'reed island'. A name which is found from time to time in Ireland.

Roger (m) Germanic, 'fame spear'. Roger was used in Ireland to anglicise *Rory*. Roger Casement (1864-1916) was an Irish patriot.

Roland [*Rólann*] (m) Germanic, 'fame land'. According to medieval legend Roland was a peer of Charlemagne who died at Roncesvalles. The Italians made the name *Orlando*, and in this form it was used by the poet Ariosto (1474-1533). It was introduced into Ireland by the English, and was occasionally used to anglicise *Revelin*. *Rowland* is a spelling variant. In fiction, the name was used in Walter Sweetman's *Roland Ryan: an Irish sketch* (1896).

Rolf [*Rodhulbh*] (m) Germanic, 'fame wolf'. A name used in medieval Ireland, but it is now rare, if not obsolete. It derives from Old German *Hrodulf* and Old Norse *Hrolfr*, whence English Rolf. The name is sometimes confused with *Ralph*.

Ronald (m) *Rögnvaldr*, a Norse name (of which *Reginald* is a modern variant) became *Raonull* amongst the Gaels of Scotland, from which came English Ronald, a name still used in modern Ireland.

Ronan [*Rónán*] (m) 'little seal'. Ronan, king of Leinster, was the subject of a tragic Irish legend. He was deceived by his second wife into killing his first son. *St Ronan's Well* (1823) was the title of a novel by Sir Walter Scott. The name is known in France, sometimes in its variant form *Renan*. It is increasingly popular in Ireland, and it has also been recorded in Canada.

Ronat (f) A name, now obsolete, derived from *ron*, 'seal'. The seal is an important animal in Celtic folklore.

Rory [*Ruairí*] (m) A derivative of *rua*, 'red, 'rufous', borne by the last high king of Ireland, Rory O'Conor (reigned 1166-70). It is still used in Ireland, and the Gaelic forms *Ruaidri*, *Ruaraidh* have been recently recorded. Rory O'More was a seventeenth-century Irish patriot. *Roderick* and *Roger* were used to anglicise Rory.

Rosaleen [*Róisín*] (f) An Irish diminutive of *Rose*. *Róisín Dubh*, 'Dark Rosaleen', was used as a figurative name for Ireland in a celebrated poem. The name is quite widespread today, often in its Irish form. Rosaleen Linehan is a contemporary Irish comedienne.

Rose [*Róis*] (f) This name generally derives from Old German *hros*, 'horse', although in the case of St Rose of Lima (1586-1617) it derives from *rosa*, 'rose', and it is almost always associated with the flower today. The forms *Rohais*, *Roese* and *Roesia* appear amongst the Normans in England, and they probably introduced the name into Ireland, where it became widespread.

Ross [*Ros*] (m) 'promontory'. A name which was common

in South Ulster. Ross MacMahon was archbishop of Armagh and a leading opponent of Cromwell. The name continues in use today.

Rossa (m) A name given in honour of Jeremiah O'Donovan Rossa, the nineteenth-century Irish politician.

Rowan [*Ruadhán*] (m) 'little red one'. An Irish name still in use today, e.g. the television reporter, Rowan Hand. Rowan can also be a Teutonic name, signifying 'mountain ash'.

Rowland (m) Variant spelling of *Roland*.

Roy (m) Gaelic *ruadh*, 'red', unconnected with French *roi*, 'king'. A name which originated in Scotland and spread from there to England and Ireland.

Ruth [*Rút*] (f) A Biblical name of unknown derivation. It is becoming increasingly popular in Ireland.

Ryan (m) 'little king'. This Irish surname is much used as a Christian name in North America, e.g. the film actor, Ryan O'Neal. It has been recorded as a Christian name in Ireland itself.

S

Sabia (f) A name used to translate *Sive*.

Sabina [*Saidhbhín*] (f) Irish *Saidhbhín*, a diminutive of *Sadhbh* (English *Sive*), became in translation *Sabina*, a Latin name meaning 'Sabine woman'. Sabina was also used to translate *Síle* (see *Sheila*).

Saibhne (m) A name, perhaps an Irish form of *Simon*, which was once used in Omeath. It is now probably obsolete.

Samantha (f) Aramaic, 'listener'. Like Darren, this name has probably spread amongst watchers of the American television series, *Bewitched*. The film *High Society* (1956) has a character Tracy Samantha Lord, played by Grace Kelly. This film may also have influenced the name's diffusion, but there is little concrete evidence of this.

Samhaoir (f) In legend, Samhaoir was Finn MacCool's daughter. It is also, in Irish, the name of the Morning Star River in Co. Limerick, and an early name for the River Erne.

Samuel (m) A Hebrew name of uncertain meaning, perhaps 'name of God'. It was used in Ireland to translate *Sorley*. Samuel is widespread in Northern Ireland. *Sam* and *Sammy* are common diminutives. Samuel Becket (1906–) the Irish writer and Nobel Prize winner is a contemporary example.

Sandra (f) This name was originally a short form of *Alessandra*, the Italian for *Alexandra*. It occurs from time to time in Ireland.

Sara(h) (f) Hebrew, 'princess'. In the Old Testament Sarah was the wife of Abraham. The name was used frequently in Ireland, sometimes to anglicise the native names *Sorcha*, *Sive* and *Saraid*.

Saraid (f) 'excellent'. This name has been anglicised as

Sarah.

Savage (m) An unusual first name used in the *Parsons* family.

Scoheen [*Scoithín*] (m) Perhaps a diminutive of *scoth*, 'flower'. St Scoheen was a sixth-century Irish saint.

Scota (f) Latin, 'Irishwoman'. Medieval legend places two women of this name amongst the progenitors of the Irish race: Scota, wife of Niul, and Scota, wife of Milesius. In the early Middle Ages *Scotia* was a name for Ireland, and *Scotus* of which Scota is the feminine, signified 'Irishman'. The term 'Scot' was applied to Irish settlers in Caledonia, who later gave their name to the whole country.

Seamus (m) The Irish form of *James,* itself derived from *Jacob. Seamus* is used by the Gaels of both Ireland and Scotland. The latter tend to favour the spelling *Seumus,* which is also found in Ireland. The vocative, *Sheamais,* is phonetically rendered by the Scots as *Hamish.* Both James and Seamus are popular names in Ireland today, though, as can happen to extremely popular names, James is no longer nearly so frequently bestowed as it once was.

James Joyce (1882-1941) was a leading Irish writer. James Connolly was an Irish rebel executed in 1916. In English the pet forms are *Jim, Jimmy (Jem, Jemser* are occasionally found in the Dublin area). *Simi* is an Irish form of Jimmy. Jimmy Kennedy was a modern Irish song-writer whose songs include *Red Sails in the Sunset* and *The Isle of Capri.*

Seamus has been phonetically rendered *Shamus* and, less successfully, *Shemus. Shay* is a frequent modern pet form. *Seamus rua* ('Red Shamus') is a name applied in Irish to the fox.

Sean (m) The Irish form of *John.* There was actually an earlier form, *Eoin* (cf. Scots Gaelic *Iain)* derived from Latin *Johannes.* The early medieval Irish philosopher, Johannes Scotus Eriugena, may have borne this form of the name. Eoin is still used today, but Sean is normally thought of as the Irish form; compare Welsh *Evan* and *Sion.* In the Gaelic-speaking areas of Scotland, Sean has not replaced *Iain,* but the lexicographer Edward Dwelly has noted it as a name which occurs in folklore there.

Sean is derived from French *Jehan/Jean,* introduced by the Normans. It is sometimes phonetically rendered in English as *Shaun* or *Shawn.* It has also been anglicised *Shane,* a form associated with Shane the Proud, chief of the *O'Neills,* a leading Irish prince in Elizabethan times.

Sean has been reinforced by *Séon,* another form of John. *Seainin,* a diminutive, is also used to name a fish, the thornback. Sean O'Casey (1880-1964), the Irish dramatist, is a recent example of the name. Sean is used outside Ireland and it has been made internationally famous by the Scottish actor, Sean Connery.

John, Sean, Eoin and Shane are all very popular today,

though John is sharply declining. John itself has been borne by a number of Irish playwrights, including John Millington Synge (1871-1909) and the contemporary playwright, John B. Keane.

Jack, the English pet form is also much employed. It comes from *Jackin,* a form of *Jankin,* itself a form of *Jehan* and *Jan* (the latter is a veriant of John). Jack Cade (died 1450) was an Irishman who led an uprising in medieval England.

Selia (f) Variant of *Sheila.*

Senan [*Séanán*] (m) A diminutive of *sean,* 'old'. *Sinon* and *Sinan* are variants.

Shamus (m) A phonetic form of *Seamus.*

Shane (m) A form of *Sean* which is used in Ireland today. Shane O'Neill (died 1567) was the principal chief of Ulster in his day.

Shannon (m, f) The name of the longest river in Ireland, which is listed by various authorities as a masculine and feminine name, but there is no evidence for its use in Ireland itself.

Sharon (f) Hebrew, 'the plain'. A name which seems well established in Ireland today.

Shasta (m) One of the various names invented by C. S. Lewis (1898-1963), the Northern Irish writer, in his Narnian chronicles. Although these names have not yet passed into common usage, they may be of interest to parents seeking unusual names for their children. The name Shasta itself may come from Mt Shasta in the United States. Other names from this series include *Caspian* (m) *Tirian* (m) *Rilian* (m) and *Aravis* (f).

Shaun (m) An alternative spelling of *Sean.*

Shauna (f) A feminine form of *Sean/Shaun.*

Shawn (m) Variant of *Sean.*

Shawndelle (f) A feminine form of *Shawn* which was coined in Canada.

Sheary (m) An Irish form of *Geoffrey.*

Sheela(gh) (f) Variant of *Sheila.*

Sheena [*Síne*] (f) The French feminine form of *John* was *Jeanne* which became *Jean* in Scotland, giving rise to Gaelic *Sin(e).* The name is also found in Ireland, particularly in the vicinity of Derry, though nowadays it has become more widespread.

Sheila [*Síle*] (f) Sile was originally an Irish form of *Cecilia, Cecily* or *Celia,* and it was variously anglicised as *Julia, Judith* and *Sabina.* However, it is chiefly in the anglicised form Sheila – or its spelling variants, *Sheela* and *Sheelagh* – that the name is used today. It remains quite common. *Selia* is a further variant. In Australia Sheila is used as a common noun to mean 'girl'.

Shelley (f) This name was originally a surname, coming from one or more of the places called Shelley in Yorkshire, Essex and Suffolk. It probably reached Ireland through the popularity of the film actress, Shelley Winters. She was, in fact, born *Shirley* – sometimes in the United States the two names are used interchangeably.

Shemus (m) A form of *Seamus*.

Sheron (m) An Irish form of *Geoffrey*, through Gaelic *Seathrun*.

Shiel [*Siadhal*] (m) An early Irish name mentioned by Woulfe; but, despite this, it has not been resurrected.

Shirley (f) English, 'shire meadow'. Originally this was a surname and masculine first name particularly associated with Yorkshire. It was probably first used as a girls' name by Charlotte Brontë in her novel *Shirley* (1849). This and recently, presumably, the fame of the film actress Shirley Temple, spread the name widely.

Shona (f) A feminine form of *John* which is sometimes found in Ireland.

Sidney (m, f) As a feminine name in Ireland this is probably a form of *Sidony*, a name once given in honour of the Winding Sheet of Christ. It is not common. Sidney is also found as a masculine name, in which case it comes from a surname which was in Latin *de Sancto Dionysio*, 'of St Denis'.

Simon [*Síomón*] (m) Greek, 'snub-nosed'. In all probability this name was equated with the Hebrew name *Simeon* (in Irish, *Suimeon*), 'hearkening'. Simon or Simeon was the original name of St Peter. Irish language variants are *Síomónn*, *Siomun* and possibly *Saibhne*. In addition, the name was used as an equivalent for *Sivney*. Simon is popular in Ireland today and the feminine form, *Simone*, sometimes also occurs.

Sinan (m) Variant of *Senan*.

Sinead (f) The Irish form of *Jane*, a common feminine of *John*. It has become very popular indeed within recent years. The actress Sinead Cusack, is a contemporary example.

Sinon (m) Variant of *Senan*.

Siobhán (f) The Irish form of *Joan* (which is sometimes rather sloppily rendered *Siún* in Irish), a name which was introduced into Ireland by the Anglo-Normans. *Siobhán* has been anglicised as *Judith* and *Julia*. Its popularity has increased greatly since mid-century. The actress, Siobhán MacKenna, is a modern example.

Sitric (m) Perhaps Norse, 'conquering security'. A name borne by medieval kings of Dublin, notably Sitric Silkenbeard. It has given rise to the surname *Kitterick*, *MacKitterick*.

Sive [*Sadhbh*] (f) 'goodness'. An early name which, over the years, has been variously anglicised as *Sabia*, *Sophia*, *Sarah*, etc. *Sabha* was a form used in Connacht; another form *Sadbha* was employed in Ulster.

Sivney [*Suibhne*] (m) 'well-going'. An early name borne by the protagonist of the medieval romance *Buile Suibhne Geilt* ('The Madness of Suibhne the Lunatic'), of which Flann O'Brien made use in his novel *At Swim-Two-Birds* (1939). Suibhne is essentially the same name as the surname *Sweeney*. It was translated as *Sivney* (formerly as *Swifne*), and sometimes anglicised as *Simon*.

Siany [*Sláine*] (f) 'health'. An early name favoured by the O'Briens. It was exported to France, where it became *Slania* and *Slanie*.

So-Domina (f) Latin *domina*, 'lady', with the Irish prefix *so-*, 'good'. A name formerly used in Ireland.

Solomon [*Solamh*] (m) A Hebrew name of uncertain meaning, which has occasionally been used in Ulster.

Sonya (f0 The Russian form of *Sophia*. Both Sonya and its spelling variant, *Sonja*, have been noted in Ireland in modern times.

Sophia (f) Greek, 'wisdom'. This name was used to anglicise the Irish name *Sive*.

Sorcha (f) An early name, which was anglicised as *Sarah*. It has once again returned into use in its own right.

Sorley [*Somhairle*] (m) Old Norse *Sumerlidi*, 'viking'. A name which was translated as *Samuel* or *Charles*. It was used amongst the *MacDonnells*, e.g., Sorley MacDonnell the Yellow, grandfather of Red Hugh O'Donnell. The name became *Somerled* in Scotland.

Standish (m) Anglo-Saxon, 'rocky valley'. This name was used to anglicise the native name *Aneslis*.

Stanislaus (m) Slavic, 'camp glory'. A name used in Ireland to anglicise *Aneslis*.

Stanley [*Stainléigh*] (m) A first name of recent origin, transferred from the surname. It is used in both Ireland and England.

Stephen [*Stiofán*] (m) Greek, 'crown'. The name of the first recorded Christian martyr (died *c.* A D 36). It was used in Ireland by the Normans, who probably introduced it to the country. There are many Irish forms: today *Stiofán* is the usual form, but in Woulfe's time *Steafán* was probably commoner. The spelling *Steven* is also found.

Susan [*Súsanna*] (f) Hebrew, 'lily'. A name introduced into Ireland by the Anglo-Normans. It has become very popular in modern times.

Suzanne (f) A form of *Susan* which is well established in Ireland.

Sybil [*Síbéal*] (f) In Ireland this name generally represents a short form of *Isabel* (cf. Early English *Zabel*) rather than *Sibyl* (sometimes spelt *Sybil*), the name applied to oracular priestesses in ancient times.

Syka (m) A form of *Eochaidh*.

Sylvester [*Sailbheastar*] (m) A derivative of Latin *silva*, 'wood'. It is occasionally found in Ireland.

Synan (m) Variant of *Senan*.

T

Taber [*Tobar*] (m) 'well'. A rare name, noted by Loughead.

Tadhg (m) 'poet'. An early name. The English forms are *Teige* and *Teague* – the latter is used as a term of opprobrium by Ulster Protestants for Catholics. The name was anglicised as *Timothy* (which accounts for the great popularity of that name in Ireland) and also as *Thaddeus, Theodore, Theodosius* and *Toby*. *Thady* is a variant form, taken from *Thaddeus*. Both Tadhg and Timothy occur in modern times. The incorrect Irish spelling *Tadgh* has also been noted. Another recorded variant is *Tighe;* and one wonders if the mysterious name *Tian,* listed by Boyer as an Irish name of uncertain meaning, is a further variant.

Tadleigh (m) Variant of *Tadhg*.

Tara [*Teamhair*] (f) The name of a hill in Central Ireland, a seat of kingship in early times, which is now used as a feminine first name. However, sometimes the name Tara may be a form of *Tamar(a)* (Hebrew, 'palm').

Teague (m) An anglicised form of *Tadhg*.

Terence (m) A Latin name of uncertain meaning, and the name of the Roman poet Terence (*c.* 195-159 BC) who was of African origin. It was used in Ireland to anglicise *Turlough* and so became very popular.

Teresa [*Toiréasa*] (f) A name meaning perhaps 'corn carrying', or possibly connected with one of the two Greek islands names Therasia. The name was once confined to Europe south of the Pyrenees, but St Teresa of Avila (1515-82) spread it far and wide. In Ireland it was identified with a native name variously rendered *Treasa* and *Treise,* meaning 'strength'. *Tracy* is a variant.

Thaddeus (m) Aramaic, 'praise'. The name of one of the Apostles, thought to be identical with St Jude. The name tended to be used more in Eastern than in Western Europe, e.g. Russian *Fadei*. In Ireland it was used to represent the native *Tadhg*.

Thady (m) A form of *Thaddeus* peculiar to Ireland, where it became widespread as an anglicisation of *Tadhg*.

Theobald [*Tiobóid*] (m) Germanic, 'people bold'. A name introduced into Ireland by the Normans. It also occurred in the form *Tibbot*. *Tioboid* has been anglicised as *Toby*. Theobald Wolfe Tone was an eighteenth-century Irish patriot.

Theodore [*Thadóir*] (m) Greek, 'gift of God'. This name was brought to Western Europe by the Venetians, although it may have existed in Wales from early times, giving rise to the Welsh name *Tewdwr*. In Ireland it was used to anglicise *Tadhg*.

Theodosius (m) Apparently a Spanish form of Greek *Theodotus*, 'God given'. It was used in Ireland to anglicise

Tadhg.

Thérèse (f) The French form of Teresa, made well known by St Thérèse of Lisieux (1873-97). It is used in Ireland today.

Thomas [*Tomás*] (m) Aramaic, 'twin'. An international name, borne by one of the Apostles, and also by St Thomas a Becket (1118-70), which made it popular amongst the Normans in Ireland. The name became widespread, but it has lost its hold recently. It has been used to anglicise *Tomhas.*

Tibbot (m) An Irish form of *Theobald,* which also occurs in Irish as *Teaboid* and *Tioboid.* The son of Grace O'Malley (see *Grania)* was called Tibbot of the Ship (he was born at sea). The form Tibbot may be of English origin as *Tibbott* was recorded in England in 1699.

Tiernan [*Tiarnán*] (m) A diminutive of *tiarna,* 'lord'.

Tierney [*Tiarnach*] (m) 'lordly'. The name of an Irish compiler of annals in the Middle Ages.

Tigris (f) Latin and Greek *tigris,* 'tiger'. By tradition St Tigris is St Patrick's sister.

Timothy (m) Greek, 'honour God'. An early Greek name, borne by a musician of Alexander the Great. It was adopted in England after the Reformation, and presumably it came from there to Ireland, where it was used to anglicise *Tadhg* and so became common. It has also been used to anglicise *Tomaltagh.* The true Irish forms are *Tiomoid* and *Tiamhdha.*

Tina (f) Originally this was a pet form of *Christina, Christine* and *Clementina,* but it is now sometimes given as an independent name.

Toal (m) Variant of *Tully.*

Toby [*Tóibí*] (m) Hebrew, 'God is good'. Toby is the usual English form of this Hebrew name. *Tobias,* another form, has been used in Ireland, e.g. a Tobias Brown of Cork was listed as a soldier of the Commonwealth. The name enjoyed considerable popularity in Europe in the Middle Ages. When it reached Ireland it was used to anglicise two names: *Tioboid* (an Irish form of *Theobald)* and *Tadhg.*

Tomaltagh [*Tomaltach*] (m) An early name which has been anglicised as *Timothy. Tumelty* is a variant.

Tomhas (m) A name used in the *O'Dowd* family, anglicised as *Thomas.*

Tracy (f) A form of *Teresa* which is sometimes used in Ireland. It has perhaps been influenced by the surname *Tracey:* indeed, *Tracey* is a spelling variant.

Tully [*Tuathal*] (m) 'people mighty'. An early name, still in use, particularly in its Irish form. *Toal* is a variant.

Tumelty (m) A form of *Tomaltagh.*

Turlough [*Toirdhealbhach*] (m) This name perhaps means 'shaped like Thor'. Thor (Irish *Tomhar)* was a Norse god whose name may be connected with 'thunder'. Turlough was the name of two kings who reigned in the tenth and eleventh centuries. Turlough I O'Brien and Turlough II O'Conor. *Tirloch* is a spelling variant. In literature, there is an Irish St Toirdhealbhach in T. H. White's *The Once and Future King* (1938-58). The name is normally pronounced *Turlock*, but the pronunciation *Traylock* sometimes occurs. It was anglicised *Terence*, which popularised that name.

Tyrone (m) An Irish name of a county in Ulster. The name signifies 'Eoghan's land' and has been used as a first name, e.g. the director Tyrone Guthrie (1900-71).

U

Uileos (m) An Irish name rendered *Ulysses* in English.

Ulicia (f) A rare feminine of *Ulick*.

Ulick [*Uileog*] (m) This name is regarded by Woulfe as a diminutive of *Uilliam*, the Irish for *William*. However, it may be a form of Norwegian *Hugleik*, 'mind reward'. *Uilleac* and *Uillioc* are variants. The name is in use today.

Ultan [*Ultán*] (m) This unusual name may be a derivative of *Ulaidh*, the Irish word for Ulster.

Ulysses (m) The Romans used the name *Ulixes*, perhaps from Etruscan *Uluxe*, for the Greek *Odysseus*, which is of uncertain meaning. They may then have used Ulysses to increase the names' resemblance to each other. In Ireland it was used to anglicise *Ulick*. James Joyce's *Ulysses* (1922) is a modern parallel of Homer's *Odyssey* set in Dublin, where Leopold Bloom takes the part of the wandering Ulysses, and Stephen Daedalus represents Telemachus, his son.

Una [*Úna*] (f) An early name, which at one stage was frequently anglicised as *Winifred*, but which is now once again popular in its own right. It was supposedly connected with *uan*, 'lamb', and it has on occasion been anglicised as *Agnes* or *Unity*. In England Una is sometimes the Latin word for 'one', taken from the character in the first book in Spenser's *Faerie Queene* (1590). However, as Spenser was resident for a time in Ireland, he may have been influenced by the Irish name. The name is pronounced *Oona* in Ireland, *Yoona* in England. *Ona, Oona(gh), Ownah* and *Wony* are variants.

Unity (f) A virtue name of the kind which became common amongst English Puritans. In Ireland it was used to anglicise the native *Una*.

Ursula (f) A diminutive of Latin *ursa*, 'she-bear'. It is quite popular in Ireland.

V

Valentine [*Vailintín*] (m) Latin, 'healthy'. A name used from time to time in Ireland, but at present it is declining. An Irish example in the seventeenth century was Valentine

Greatrakes, who was reputed to be able to heal scrofula by touch.

Valerie (f) The French form of the Latin name *Valeria*, 'healthy'. It is sometimes found in Ireland today.

Vanessa (f) A name invented by the Irish writer, Jonathan Swift (1667-1745), to use for Esther Vanhomrigh. It has now spread beyond the shores of Ireland – the English actress, Vanessa Redgrave (1937–), has probably helped with its recent dissemination – and it is used quite frequently in Britain, Canada and Australia. Yonge, writing in the last century, does not mention it at all, indicating that it became widespread only in modern times.

Veronica (f) Latin, 'true image'. A name sometimes found in Ireland. It is given out of reverence for Veronica who is supposed to have wiped the face of Christ on the way to His Crucifixion.

Vevina (f) A form of the Gaelic name *Bébhinn* ('sweet lady') used by Macpherson in his Ossianic poems (1765).

Victor (m) Latin, 'conqueror'. A name which was more or less confined to Italy in the form *Vittore*, until after the French Revolution. It came into use in England in the nineteenth century (isolated examples had occurred before). Queen Victoria's similar name may have had an influence, though *Victoria* is not the feminine of Victor: it is the feminine of *Victorius*. In Ireland, Victor was used to anglicise *Buagh*.

Victoria [*Victeoiria*] (f) Latin, 'victory'. A name introduced into Ireland from England, where it came into general use only in the nineteenth century. Quite popular around 1900, it later declined, as it was considered too English in a time of Nationalist fervour. However, it is now making a comeback.

Vincent [*Uinseann*] (m) Latin, 'conquering'. This name was brought to Ireland by the Normans. The French priest St Vincent de Paul (1576-1669) probably added to its popularity. *Uinsionn* is a variant Irish form. It now seems to be used less and less.

Vivienne (f) Latin, 'living'. This name originally sprang up in the French language, perhaps due to confusion with Celtic *Ninian*. *Vivian*, another form, was used in Ireland to anglicise *Bébhinn* ('sweet lady') of which *Bevin* is the true translation. Vivian has also been recorded as a masculine name in Ireland.

W

Walter [*Ualtar*] (m) Germanic, 'rule folk'. The name of a prince of Aquitaine in legend, which was introduced to Ireland by the Normans. *Thaiter* was a peculiar Irish form, which now seems obsolete.

Walters [*Bhaltair*] (m) A variant of *Walter* borne by one, Bhaltair O'Toole, in the twelfth century. His name was variously translated as Walters and Walter.

Whiltierna [*Faoiltiarna*] (f) An early name, a combination of *faol*, 'wolf', and *tiarna*, 'lord', which sounds somewhat masculine for a woman's name.

William [*Liam*] (m) Germanic, 'will helmet'. A name frequently used by the Normans in medieval Ireland. It became very popular and remains so today. In Irish it became first *Uilliam*, then it was contracted to *Liam*. In modern times William is more frequently bestowed than the Irish Liam. William Butler Yeats (1865-1839) was an influential playwright and poet.

Winfred (m) This unusual name appears to be used in Ireland as a masculine form of *Winifred*. Indeed, Winifred itself was registered as a masculine name in Cork at the turn of the century. The name is unlikely to be connected with the Teutonic name *Winfred*, 'friend peace'.

Winifred (f) A name derived from *Wenefreda*, the Latin form of Welsh *Grewfrwei*, 'blessed reconciliation'. In Ireland it was used to anglicise the native name *Una*, perhaps because Una had a variant *Wony* which may have been thought identical with *Winnie*, the pet form of Winifred. As Winifred becomes less popular in modern Ireland, Una becomes more so.

Withypoll (f) This curious name, which may well be peculiar to Ireland, occurs in the pedigree of the *Losse* family of Dublin. It possibly comes from English *withy*, 'twig', 'willow' and *poll*, 'head'.

Wony (f) A form of *Una*.

Y

Y (m) This must surely be one of the world's shortest names. Actually, it is a form of *Aodh* which occurs in fifteenth-century documents.

Yseult (f) Variant of *Iseult*.

Ysolte (f) Variant of *Iseult*.

Yvonne (f) A French name, ultimately Germanic, signifying 'yew'. It is now fairly common in Ireland. *Evonne*, a possible variant, was registered in Ireland in 1975, and *Yvette*, a cognate name, also occurs.

Z

Zaira (f) This name was invented by the Irish writer C. R. Maturin, who used it in his novel *Women; or, pour et contre* (1818).

Zephan (m) This name is listed by Weidenham as that of an Irish saint.

Zinna (f) An unusual feminine name which occurs in the *Toler-Aylward* family of Shankhill Castle.

Bibliography

Attwater, D., *Names and Name-Days* (London, 1939).

Boyer, C., *Names for Girls and Boys* (St Albans, 1974).

Brown, S. J., *Ireland in Fiction, Volume 1* (Dublin, 1919).

Burke, B., *Burke's Genealogical and Heraldic History of the Landed Gentry of Ireland* (London,1958).

Byrne, F. J., *Irish Kings and High Kings* (London, 1973).

Cross, T. P., and Slover, C., *Ancient Irish Tales* (Dublin, 1969).

De Bhaldraithe, T., *English-Irish Dictionary* (Dublin, 1959).

Dinnen, P. S., *An Irish-English Dictionary* (Dublin, 1927).

Dunkling, L. A., *First Names First* (London, 1977).

Gaelic Journal (Periodical).

Kolacht, A. J., *The Name Dictionary* (New York, 1967).

Lane, T. O'N., *Larger English-Irish Dictionary* (Dublin, 1921).

Loughead, F, H., *Dictionary of Given Names* (Glendale, 1974).

MacLysaght, E., *The Surnames of Ireland* (Shannon, 1969).

Matheson, R. E., *Varieties and Synonymes of Surnames and Christian Names in Ireland* (Dublin, 1901).

Neeson, E., *The Book of Irish Saints* (Cork, 1967).

New Ireland Review (Periodical).

Nurnberg, M., and Rosenblum, M., *What to Name your Baby* (New York, 1962).

O'Hart, J., *The Irish and Anglo-Irish Landed Gentry* (Dublin, 1884).

O'Hart, J., *Irish Pedigrees* (New York, 1915).

Rule, L., *Name Your Baby* (New York, 1963).

Sleigh, L., and Johnson, C., *The Pan Book of Boys' Names* (London, 1965).

Sleigh, L., and Johnson, C., *The Pan Book of Girls' Names* (London, 1965).

Spence, H., *The Modern Book of Babies' Names* (London, 1975).

Transactions of the Gaelic Society of Inverness (Periodical).

Weidenham, J. L., *Baptismal Names* (Baltimore, 1931).

Withycombe, E. G., *The Oxford Dictionary of English Christian Names* (Oxford, 1977).

Woulfe, P., *Irish Names for Children* (Dublin, 1974).

Yonge, C. M., *History of Christian Names* (London, 1884).